Learning UNIX with examples

4^{thrd} EDITION

David Martínez Perales

All trademarks mentioned in this book, belong to their owners.

The aim of this publication is to learning and lack of accountability in the use of the reader to information he provided.

All Rights Reserved published in any language to its author, David Martínez Perales.

No part of this book may be reproduced by any means, as stipulated in the penal code.

ISBN: 978-1-291-40791-4
Editor: Lulu.com
Property rights: David Martínez Perales
Copyright: © 2013
Language: English
Country: Spain

This book is dedicated to everyone who helped me gain the knowledge of computer science that have made it possible to write this book. Of course, I would also like to dedicate my wife Raquel, my family and my friends.

INDEX

Part 1 13
Basic knowledges of UNIX...13
Introduction..15
History of UNIX..15
What is a computer system?..16
    Definition and concepts...16
    The binary system..17
        Transactions in binary numbers..18
        From binary to decimal conversion...19
        From decimal to binary conversion...19
    Octal and hexadecimal numbering systems...20
        From binary to octal conversion..21
        From binary to hexadecimal conversion...21
Learn to move through the operating system..23
Introduction..23
Login..24
How do you run a command?..25
    Modify the standard output of a command..26
Editing text files..27
    The vi editor...27
        Edit text..27
        Display control...28
        Clear text...28
        Search..29
        Others..29
Basic commands related to the file system...34
    Show the files it contains a directory...37
    Create a directory 37
    Enter and exit a directory...38
    knowing the current directoy...38
    View the contents of a text file 38
    Copy a file to another directoy...39
    Delete a file..39
    Move and rename a file...40
    Create a link to a file 40
    Synchronize file systems...41
    Find a file 41
    Pack and unpack an archive in tar format...43
    Compress and decompress a file 44
    Knowing the available space in the current directory 45

Find out which files and directories are larger..46
Know what processes are using a file system..47
Knowing what type is a file..48
Translate to text a binary file 48
Run an application using the graphical mode...49
    xhost..50
    XAuth..51
Basic commands related to the processes..51
    Knowing the processes that are running on the system 53
    Reviewing the consumption of CPU and memory each process 54
    Forcing the completion of a process 56
    Capture the signal of completion of a process 58
    Modify the priority of execution of a process..59
    Knowing the time of execution of a process 59
    Running processes in background 60
    Planning tasks with cron 61
    Reviewing the processes that are running users connected..............................63
Basic commands related to the filters...63
    Search for text strings 64
    Sort strings 66
    Remove the repeated lines of a text..67
    Lines, words and characters counter 68
    Cut characters from a text string 69
    Replace a string by another 70
    See the first few lines of text 70
    See the last lines of a text 71
    Compare the contents of two text files...71
Part 2...73
UNIX administration knowledges...73
Administration of UNIX systems...74
Introduction..74
What happens during the boot of the operating system?..74
    inittab and runlevels..75
Users and groups administration...79
    Concepts...79
    Add a group to the system 80
    Create an user account 81
    Deleting a user 81
    Deleting a group 82
    Modify a user's password 82
    Managing groups 82
    Get the user identifiers and group membership for a user 83

Switch user 83
Searching for errors in the configuration files of passwords and groups 84
Use a different shell from the current 85
Managing permissions on files and directories...86
Modify the permissions of reading, writing and execution of a file 86
Permission setuid 90
Permission setgid 91
Permission sticky-bit 91
Changing the group and owner of a file 92
sudo configuration..93
File system administration...98
Concepts..98
Creating a partition, a file system, mount the file system and use it........................99
Create the entry of a new device in the system 106
Network Filesystem Service (NFS)..106
Disks in mirror..108
   Concepts..108
   Creating a mirror structure by software...109
   RAID5..110
Logical Volume Manager (LVM)...111
   Concepts..111
   Creating a LVM structure...116
   LVM commands..117
      Expand a file system...117
      Modify the properties of a logical volume..117
      Create a logical volume..117
      Deleting a logical volume...118
      Show information of the logical volumes..118
      Creating a mirror of a logical volume..118
      Deleting a mirror..118
      Synchronize two LVS in mirror...118
      Increasing the size of a logical volume...118
      Decreasing the size of a logical volume..118
      Create a physical volume...118
      Remove a physical volume..119
      Modify the properties of a physical volume...119
      Check the consistency of a physical volume..119
      Save the settings of LVM...119
      Restore the LVM configuration...119
      Create a VG..119
      Remove a VG of the system..119
      Removes a group of volumes in the system and its associated disks............120

Activate or deactivate a VG	120
Show the configuration of a VG	120
Add a disk to a VG	120
Importing a VG to a system	120
Remove a disk from a VG	120
Move a VG from one server to another	120
Network administration	**122**
Concepts	122
Some of the most important hardware elements:	122
The elements of software that can be found:	122
Assembly and operation of a network structure	123
IP	125
Netmask	126
Broadcast addresses	128
Domain Name Server (DNS)	129
Gateway	130
Loopback IP	130
Dynamic Host Configuration Protocol (DHCP)	131
MAC Address	131
Communications port	131
Network configuration on a UNIX system	134
Configure a network card	134
Gateway configuration	136
DNS configuration	136
Virtual IP configuration	137
Delete the configuration of a network interface	138
Configuring an interface bridge	139
ARP tables	140
Other commands system linked to computer networks	141
ping	141
traceroute	141
netstat	142
hostname	144
domainname	145
nslookup	146
telnet	146
ssh	146
finger	147
talk	147
rpcinfo	147
The proxy squid	**148**
Concepts	148

| squid configuration..149
| File Transfer Protocol (FTP)..153
| Concepts..153
| Examples of the use of FTP commands..155
| FTP server configuration...158
| Jail FTP users to their home directory...160
| Secure connections...163
| Secure Shell (SSH)..163
| Creation of the public and private keys..163
| Establishing a relationship of trust between keys.................................165
| Establishing a relationship of trust based on user-host relationship...................166
| Copy a local file to a remote server..167
| Export an environment variable remotely.....................................167
| Redirection of local ports...168
| Redirection of remote ports..168
| Secure FTP (SFTP)...169
| Automating a SFTP connection..170
| CHROOT directories..171
| Secure Sockets Layer (SSL)..172
| Concepts..173
| Generating a digital certificate...175
| Creating the file that openssl will use to generate the certificate with the relevant information...175
| Creating the file with the public key...176
| Creating the "local" certificate..177
| Sign our own certificate..180
| Check the certificate...181
| Configuring the Webserver to use the certificate generated......................184
| The mail server sendmail..185
| Concepts..185
| Configuring a mail server..186
| Masking...193
| Message queue...193
| Relay...193
| Time synchronization via NTP..195
| The printing system...198
| PostScript..198
| Commands related to the printing system...199
| SAMBA-CIFS..202
| Shell script..209
| Interprets of commands..209
| Ways to run a script..211

    Reserved variables..212
    Functions of the shell..214
        shift number 214
        read variables 215
        expr 216
        test 217
        if 219
        case 220
        while 221
        until 223
        for...223
        break, continue and exit..226
        select 227
        Use of arrays..229
    Functions created by us...230
    Save useful information generated by a script..234
High availability systems..236
    Concepts...236
    What is a cluster of applications?..236
    How is it possible that two servers have access to the same disks of the tower?....238
    Configuring a cluster...242
Relationship of commands, and other peculiarities between different UNIX systems 248
Memory Usage..264

Part 1

Basic knowledges of UNIX

Introduction

History of UNIX

Today, UNIX operating system is a multi-user, multitasking, portable, with different command interpreters, multiprocessor, multi core, with compilers, with a graphical environment... among many other features that define it, according to the *The Open Group*. This institution is a group of leading companies in UNIX technology as HP or IBM, among others, who are responsible for granting standards in various branches of computer science.

UNIX is a derivative of what originally was called UNICS (***Uni**plexed **I**nformation and **C**omputing **S**ystem*). This project was aimed at creating a single operating system, whose result was the creation of UNICS, which ended in UNIX because a play on words in which they do not go into detail. This system was invented in the 60s by Bell Laboratories of AT & T, through a team of Ken Thompson and Dennis Ritchie, among others. The first version of the system was written in assembly language, but the needs of portability to other hardware architectures made to change this language for C, much more friendly to assembler (machine code).

During the decades of the '70s and '80s, UNIX was taking popular among various academic institutions through licenses distributed by its creators. This, together with the ease that provided C to make changes in the source code, favoured to their rapid development and therefore commercial use. Currently, there are two variants of UNIX systems:

- The arm of AT & T, which would become the System V.
- The branch of Berkley or BSD, developed by the University of California.

Some of the most UNIX systems that are used today, are:

- AIX, this is a commercial Unix based in System V, developed by IBM in February 1990.
- **Sun Solaris**, commercial Unix based in System *V* and *BSD* developed by *SUN Microsystems.*
- **HP-UX**, commercial Unix based in *BSD* developed by *Hewlett Packard* from 1986.
- **Ultrix**, commercial UNIX developed by *DEC*.
- **IRIX**, commercial UNIX developed by *SGI*.
- **Unixware**, commercial UNIX developed by *Novell*.
- **Unix SCO**, commercial UNIX based in *System V* developed by *Santa Cruz Operations* and *Hewlett Packard* from 1979.
- **Tru64 UNIX**, commercial UNIX developed by *Compaq*.
- **Linux,** There are a variety of Linux distributions. Among the highlights are: RedHat, Fedora, Suse, Debian, Ubuntu, Mandriva and Gentoo, although there are many more in the market, and as specializing http://distrowatch.com/ Web pages that provide information on the different systems. There are versions of pay, free software and a variety of good and completely free**.**

What is a computer system?

Definition and concepts

A computer system is the set of hardware, software and the human team that can interact with this association.

The hardware components are all physical and electronic components that are part of the overall system. There are various types and functions: from the basics such as CPU, memory, hard drives, keyboard, monitor, until the communication elements such as routers, switches, firewalls and cabling, to name but a few.

Of all the hardware components we can highlight two of them:

- The **CPU** (Central Processing Unit) is the most important element of a computer system. We could say that is the brain of a computer because it is responsible for doing all the mathematical calculations of the orders it receives.
- The **memory** device is the hardware on which you can read and write data accessed by the processor (CPU) in a way very fast. All data contained in it are temporary.

The software programs are all able to use the hardware to perform their tasks. There are a wide variety of programs: word processors, spreadsheets, planners tasks, drawing tools, web browsers, the operating system itself, compilers of source code to create other programs...

What happens after a user submits an order until it sees its result is to write a book full of individual parts that interact, which means it is not our aim, however, we will try to summarize with the following schema:

1. The user of an application sends an order, for example, from the keyboard.
2. The data associated with the instruction they travelled to the physical memory of the computer through a data bus.
3. The processor accesses the memory to read the information stored in it and, thus, be able to execute mathematical calculations associated with the order given and send, via the data bus, the corresponding result to the peripheral, such as a screen or to the hard drive to store any file, form example.

The current systems use the binary system for all its operations.

The binary system

Humans are accustomed to using the decimal system to represent any figure by the numbers ranging from 0 to 9, however, in the binary system is used only 0 and 1, for that reason, also called logical system (yes / no).

Because the computers run with electricity and have to be able to solve mathematical operations, in a logical 0 occurs with the absence of electric voltage, while 1 is in the opposite situation.

By way of curiosity, commenting that this system exists since before we invented electricity and comes from the Hindu culture.

Transactions in binary numbers

Sum:

    0 + 0 = 0
    0 + 1 = 1
    1 + 0 = 1
    1 + 1 = 10 ← This is not the number ten in decimal. These numbers are one and zero binaries

Subtraction:

    0 – 0 = 0
    1 – 0 = 1
    1 – 1 = 0
    0 – 1 = It uses the system as a "drag" on the decimal system, that is, taking a unit provided the following position.

Multiplication:

    0 x 0 = 0
    0 x 1 = 0
    1 x 0 = 0
    1 x 1 = 1

Division:

It is a recursive subtraction.

Example:

```
101010 / 110
-110      111
 1010
 -110
  0110
  -110
   000
```

From binary to decimal conversion

Each digit, individually, have been multiplied by two raised to the power "x", where "x" is the position of the digit starting from the right and zero the first of the values. After calculating each of the digits, must to add all the results obtained. An example would be clearer:

Position	3	2	1	0
Digits	1	0	1	1

1 x 2 raised to 0 = 1
1 x 2 raised to 1 = 2
0 * 2 raised to 2 = 0
1 * 2 raised to 3 = 8

The resulting number is the sum of all previous calculations: 11

From decimal to binary conversion

You have to divide the decimal number by two until the result is an indivisible number.

Example:

    100|0
    50 |0
    25 |1 → 1, 25-1=24 and we continue dividing by two
    12 |0
    6 |0
    3 |1
    1 |1

Octal and hexadecimal numbering systems

There are other numbering systems that are used very frequently in the world of computing. They are the octal and hexadecimal. Their base changes are as follows:

Decimal number	Binary representation	Octal representation	Hexadecimal representation
0	0	0	0
1	1	1	1
2	10	2	2
3	11	3	3
4	100	4	4
5	101	5	5
6	110	6	6
7	111	7	7
8	1000	10	8
9	1001	11	9
10	1010	12	A (Decimal value =

			10)
11	1011	13	B
12	1100	14	C
13	1101	15	D
14	1110	16	E
15	1111	17	F
16	10000	20	10

From binary to octal conversion

Divide the number of 12 binary digits in groups of three, and we associate the octal value of each group:

    100   011   010   001
      4   3   2   1

From binary to hexadecimal conversion

The binary number is divided into groups of four bits and we associate their hexadecimal representation to each group:

    1000   1101   0001
      8   D   1

Learn to move through the operating system

Introduction

To be able to start using a UNIX system, you must have a user or an account in the operating system. This account will provide us the system administrator, as well as the way we have to connect to it, that is, we need:

- <u>IP server:</u> It is a unique address that identifies the server that we want to connect in a network.
- <u>Connection type:</u> Secure or not secure. If the administrator tells us that we need to access to the server thought a NOT secure connection, he will be saying to us that we will have to go through *telnet*. If the connection is secure, we will use SSH. A secure connection means that the traffic of packages that are circulating in the network between our computer and the remote server, is so encrypted in order to prevent the theft of information, such as a password, for example.
- <u>The communications port:</u> Although it is not usual for security issues, some administrators prefer to modify the standard connection port for a custom.

Login

Imagine that the data that our system administrator has given us are:

- IP server: 7.2.1.144
- Connection type: Enabled the secure and not secure.
- Communication port: Standard
- Account name: user1

To be able to connect, we need a client software that allows us connect to the server. The standard commands of UNIX systems are:

- No secure connection: telnet IP_of_the_remote_server. In our case, the command that we would be typing is: *telnet 7.2.1.144*.
- Secure connection: ssh -p port account@IP_of_the_remote_server. In our case, we would execute the instruction *ssh 7.2.1.144* or ssh *user1@7.2.1.144* or *ssh -l user1@7.2.1.144*.

If we are accessing, for example, from a Windows system, we can also type the telnet command to connect for the not secure connection and an applications as Secure CRT or *putty*, for the secure. Once typed either of the above commands, the system we asked the user name and password that gave us the administrator.

Example:

[server1] user1:/home/user1 $ ssh root@server2
ssh-keysign not enabled in /opt/ssh/etc/ssh_config
ssh_keysign: no reply
key_sign failed
Password:
Last successful login for root: Thu Dec 4 10:04:33 MET-1METDST 2008 on pts/ta
Last unsuccessful login for root: Fri Nov 21 13:52:02 MET-1METDST 2008
Last login: Wed Dec 3 12:47:51 2008 from caiasp03
(c)Copyright 1983-2003 Hewlett-Packard Development Company, L.P.
(c)Copyright 1979, 1980, 1983, 1985-1993 The Regents of the Univ. of California
(c)Copyright 1980, 1984, 1986 Novell, Inc.
(c)Copyright 1986-2000 Sun Microsystems, Inc.
(c)Copyright 1985, 1986, 1988 Massachusetts Institute of Technology

(c)Copyright 1989-1993 The Open Software Foundation, Inc.
(c)Copyright 1990 Motorola, Inc.
(c)Copyright 1990, 1991, 1992 Cornell University
(c)Copyright 1989-1991 The University of Maryland
(c)Copyright 1988 Carnegie Mellon University
(c)Copyright 1991-2003 Mentat Inc.
(c)Copyright 1996 Morning Star Technologies, Inc.
(c)Copyright 1996 Progressive Systems, Inc.

          RESTRICTED RIGHTS LEGEND
Use, duplication, or disclosure by the U.S. Government is subject to
restrictions as set forth in sub-paragraph (c)(1)(ii) of the Rights in
Technical Data and Computer Software clause in DFARS 252.227-7013.

        Hewlett-Packard Company
        3000 Hanover Street
        Palo Alto, CA 94304 U.S.A.

Rights for non-DOD U.S. Government Departments and Agencies are as set
forth in FAR 52.227-19(c)(1,2).
You have mail.

Value of TERM has been set to "vt100".
WARNING: YOU ARE SUPERUSER !!

[server2] root:/root #

How do you run a command?

We have several ways to execute commands:

- Command & → Run the command in background. Later in the chapter "Commands related processes," we explain this and other ways of running processes in background.
- Command1 ; Command2; CommandN → Execute all commands separated by a

semicolon. The advantage is that is that we do in one line. It is useful to avoid having to wait to take control of the shell again before typing the next instruction.
- Command1 | Command2 → The output from the first command is the entry of the second. It is very useful in use with filters, as will be seen in the chapter "Basic commands related to the filters." The symbol "|" is called a pipe.
- Command `Command2` → The output of the second command, is used as a parameter of the first.
- Command1 && Command2 → If the first command ends successfully, you execute the second.

Modify the standard output of a command

By default, when you run an instruction we see its result by its standard output, that is, if we want to see the files that contains a directory, *ls* we show them at the screen, or whether we send to print a file, its output will be the printer, but there are cases that we are interested in changing the standard output. To take one simple example, you may want to save the information on the contents of directory in a file rather than see the result on screen. This is called redirection.

- Input redirection: We get information from a file rather than, for example, the keyboard.

    Example:

    ➢ Instead of typing the contents of an e-mail, we get the text of a file:

    mail < myfile.txt

- Output redirection: We sent the information obtained with a command to an exit different from the standard.

    Example:

    ➢ The file *content.txt* saves the information it obtains the command *ls-la*. This information would be displayed if not we would have redirected:

```
ls -la > content.txt
```

- The file *content.txt* also saves the information obtained by the command who, but is added at the end of the file without deleting the information above:

```
who >> content.txt
```

Once defined the basic concepts for the execution of the commands, we can begin with the practices.

In order to build and modify the examples that come in this book, we will start by explaining how to edit a text file.

Editing text files

In UNIX systems there are a multitude of applications for editing texts ranging from the most complex as the Openoffice up that were created during the birth of the first UNIX versions, such as *vi*. This editor is installed on all versions of UNIX and that is why we will explain below.

The vi editor

This section explains the basic functions of the command. To run we will type *vi* or *vi file_name*.

Once we are under the control of this software, we can use the following instructions (some of them depend on the product version you have installed):

- Edit text
    - i → Insert text before the cursor.
    - I → Insert to the top of the line.

a → We insert after the cursor.
A → Insert at the end of the line.
R → Replace text (overwrite).
yy → Copy the current line and inserts it at the next.

- Cursor movement

    Arrows → We are moving in different directions.
    h or BS → We are moving to the left.
    l or SP → We are moving to the right.
    k or - → Come one line upward.
    j or + → Come on down a line.
    $ → We move at the end of the current line.
    0 → Come to the top of the line.
    11G → We are going to the line 11.
    Ctrl-G → Shows the number of current line.
    w → We are placed in the beginning of the next word.
    e → Come the end of the following word.
    b → The cursor moves to the top of the previous word.
    ^ → We are placed in the first word of the line.
    H → We are going to the top of the screen.
    L → We are at the bottom of the screen.

- Display control

    Ctrl-f → Advance page.
    Ctrl-b → Backward page.

- Clear text

    x → Delete the character where we are located.
    X (Backspace) → Deletes characters back.
    dd → Delete the current line.
    D → Remove from the cursor to the end of the line.
    dw → Remove from the cursor to the end of a word.
    d$ → Remove from the cursor to the end of the line.
    d0 → Remove from the cursor to the top of the line.

- Search

    /*text* → Search forward.
    ?*text* → Search backward.
    n → Repeat the last search.

- Replacement

    c → Replace characters.
    r → Replace a character.
    cw → Same as above but with words.
    :<from>,<to>s/<search>/<replacement>/g → Find and replace a word.

- Others

    J → The next line joins the current forming a single line.
    u → Undo last action.
    ESC → It allows to run the commands of vi, leaving the current one.
    :q → We left vi if we have not made any changes.
    :q! → Exit without saving.
    :w → Save changes.
    :w *file1* → Save the changes to the file *file1*.
    :wq → Save changes and exit.
    . (point) → Repeats the last action.

Example of creating a text file with *vi*:

1. We execute *vi*:

```
[usuario1@rd00 ~]$ vi
```

2. Appears the edition text screen:

```
                        VIM - VI Mejorado

                         versión 7.3.56
                      por Bram Moolenaar et al.
                   Modificado por <bugzilla@redhat.com>
              Vim es código abierto y se puede distribuir libremente

                    ¡Ayude a los niños pobres de Uganda!
              escriba  «:help iccf<Intro>»    para más información

              escriba  «:q<Intro>»                para salir
              escriba  «:help<Intro>» o <F1>  para obtener ayuda
         escriba «:help version7<Intro>» para información de la versión


                                                         0,0-1        Todo
```

3. We press the "i" key to insert text:

```
                        VIM - VI Mejorado

                         versión 7.3.56
                      por Bram Moolenaar et al.
                   Modificado por <bugzilla@redhat.com>
              Vim es código abierto y se puede distribuir libremente

                    ¡Ayude a los niños pobres de Uganda!
              escriba  «:help iccf<Intro>»    para más información

              escriba  «:q<Intro>»                para salir
              escriba  «:help<Intro>» o <F1>  para obtener ayuda
         escriba «:help version7<Intro>» para información de la versión




-- INSERTAR --                                           0,1          Todo
```

4. We write a text message:

5. We save the document throutht the key combinations *w FileName*.

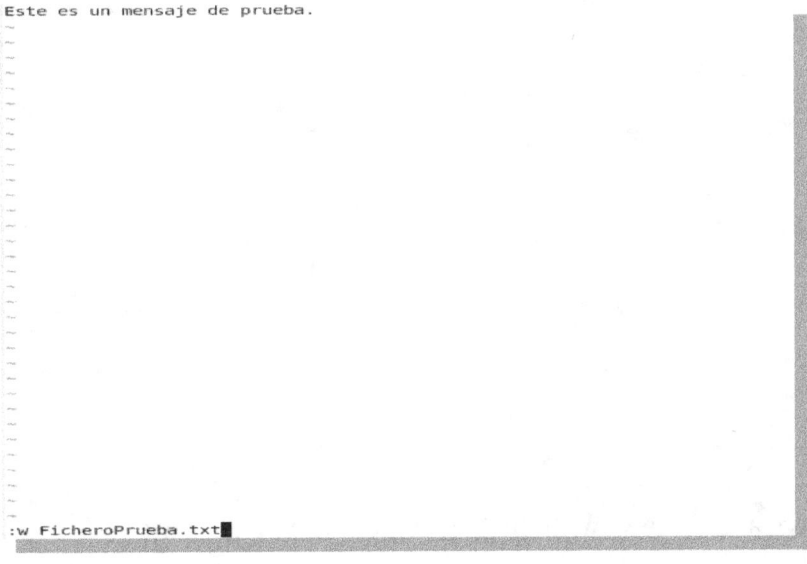

```
Este es un mensaje de prueba.
~
~
~
...
~
"FicheroPrueba.txt" [Nuevo] 1L, 30C escritos
```

6. We press the key combination *Shift A* to put us at the end of the line and continue editing the file:

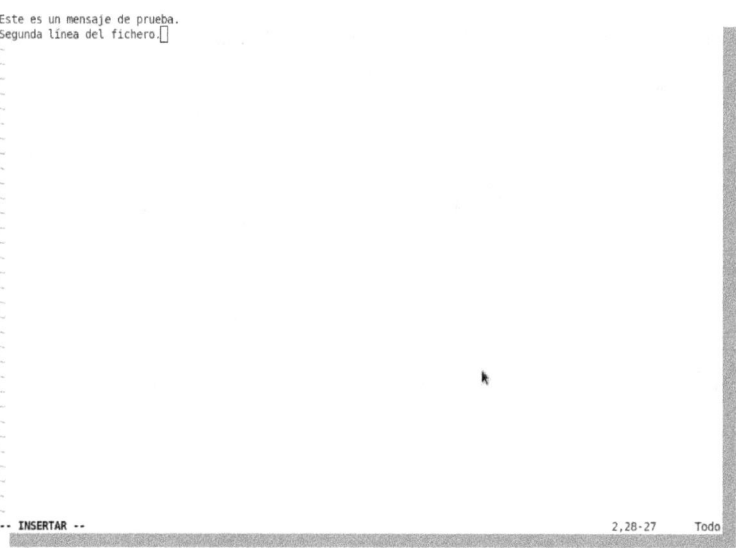

7. We save and close vi with the key combination *ESC : w q*

```
Este es un mensaje de prueba.
Segunda línea del fichero.
~
~
~
~
~
~
~
~
~
~
~
~
~
~
~
~
~
~
~
~
~
~
~
~
~
~
~
:wq
```

8. Now we check that the file exists and contains everything we have written:

[usuario1@rd00 ~]$ ls -la FicheroPrueba.txt
-rw-rw-r-- 1 usuario1 usuario1 58 abr 16 17:20 FicheroPrueba.txt
[usuario1@rd00 ~]$ cat FicheroPrueba.txt
Este es un mensaje de prueba.
Segunda línea del fichero.
[usuario1@rd00 ~]$

Basic commands related to the file system

The basic operation of UNIX is done through files. Directories, software, printers, modems, etc. are treated as files on UNIX systems.

Each system can be configured in a thousand different ways, but there is a convention with regard to information that is stored and in what place:

- **/dev** → It contains the files of devices, such as the location of a printer or a hard disk.

- **/var** → Variable information. It contains the following subdirectories (may vary depending on the system that we are using):

    adm: Administrative information system.
    lib: the status of applications.
    local: Variable information software of /usr/local.
    log: Historic system - system errors, hardware, informational, and so on. The daemon syslogd must to be started for the logs are saved in the files listed in the *syslog.conf*.
    named: DNS files.
    nis: NIS database files.
    run: Files related to running processes.
    spool: Directories of jobs that are in the queue waiting to be executed.
    tmp: Temporary files.

- **/usr** → They are the working directories of users of the system. It contains the following subdirectories:

    X11Rx: X Window System Version 11 release "x".
    bin: Programs no natives of the system.
    etc: System configuration.
    include: Header files included by C programs.
    lib: Libraries → LD_LIBRARY_PATH - is the environment variable that contains the paths of libraries.
    local: The system administrator adds its own local configuration of the system.
    man: Manuals command.
    sbin: Binary of the management system.

src: Source code.

- **/opt** → It is used as the destination directory to install the applications. This directory can also be found in /var as a subdirectory.

- **/proc** → It stores information about the system (type of information, loaded kernel modules ...).

Before you start to type commands, you should know that there is one that we are going to be a big help, even when we are expert managers. Is the command *man [command]*. It gives us a detailed description of each command and what is it for each of its parameters.

Example of help of *ls* instruction:

[user1@noname00 ~]$ man ls

LS(1)   User Commands   LS(1)

NAME
    ls - list directory contents

SYNOPSIS
    ls [OPTION]... [FILE]...

DESCRIPTION
       List information about the FILEs (the current directory by default). Sort entries alphabetically if none of -cftuvSUX nor --sort.

    Mandatory arguments to long options are mandatory for short options too.

    -a, --all
        do not ignore entries starting with .

    -A, --almost-all
        do not list implied . and ..

    --author

with -l, print the author of each file
-b, --escape
    print octal escapes for nongraphic characters

--block-size=SIZE
    use SIZE-byte blocks

-B, --ignore-backups
    do not list implied entries ending with ~

-c   with -lt: sort by, and show, ctime (time of last modification of file status information) with -l: show ctime and sort by name otherwise: sort by
    ctime
-C   list entries by columns

--color[=WHEN]
    control whether color is used to distinguish file types. WHEN may be 'never', 'always', or 'auto'

-d, --directory
    list directory entries instead of contents, and do not dereference symbolic links

-D, --dired
    generate output designed for Emacs' dired mode

-f   do not sort, enable -aU, disable -ls --color

-F, --classify
    append indicator (one of */=>@|) to entries

--file-type
    likewise, except do not append '*'

--format=WORD
        across -x, commas -m, horizontal -x, long -l, single-column -1, verbose -l, vertical -C

--full-time
    like -l --time-style=full-iso

    -g   like -l, but do not list owner
The basic tasks that a user needs to know to move through the system are as follows:

Show the files it contains a directory

To do this, we use the *ls* command.

Example:

```
[user1@noname00 ~]$ ls -la
total 12
drwx------ 4 user1 user1  88 oct 27 19:29 .
drwxr-xr-x 6 root  root   61 oct 27 19:29 ..
-rw-r--r-- 1 user1 user1  18 feb 29  2008 .bash_logout
-rw-r--r-- 1 user1 user1 176 feb 29  2008 .bash_profile
-rw-r--r-- 1 user1 user1 124 feb 29  2008 .bashrc
drwxr-xr-x 2 user1 user1   6 abr  6  2008 .gnome2
drwxr-xr-x 4 user1 user1  37 may 30 22:17 .mozilla
[user1@noname00 ~]$
```

Create a directory

It is a structure of the file system used for grouping data.

Example:

```
[user1@noname00 ~]$ mkdir contacts
[user1@noname00 ~]$ ls -l
total 0
drwxrwxr-x 2 user1 user1 6 oct 27 19:40 contacts
[user1@noname00 ~]$
```

You can create so many directories and subdirectories as you want.

Enter and exit a directory

Example:

> Enter

[user1@noname00 ~]$ cd contacts
[user1@noname00 contacts]$ ls
vocals.txt
[user1@noname00 contacts]$

> Exit

[user1@noname00 contacts]$ cd ..
[user1@noname00 ~]$

knowing the current directoy

Example:

[user1@noname00 contacts]$ pwd
/home/user1/contacts
[user1@noname00 contacts]$

Knowing the full path, we could use the *cd* command like c*d /home/user1/contacts*.

View the contents of a text file

cat, more or *vi* are some commands dedicated to this function.

Example:

```
[user1@noname00 contacts]$ cat vocals.txt
a, e, i, o, u
[user1@noname00 contacts]$
```

Copy a file to another directoy

Example:

```
[user1@noname00 contacts]$ cp -p vocals.txt /home/user1/letters
[user1@noname00 contacts]$ ls /home/user1/letters/
vocals.txt
[user1@noname00 contacts]$
```

With the parameter *-p* we retain the original permissions of the file and its date of creation.

To do this remotely, that is to say, from one system to another we have the rcp command. This command is obsolete because it does not use a secure connection. To use it, is necessary that the rsh (/usr/bin/rsh) service is running and at in the file $HOME/.rhosts of the destination server is included the **fixed** IP of the origin server, because this is the IP to communicate to the remote server.

Example:

```
[user1@noname00 ~]$ rcp test.txt user2@server2:test.txt
```

Delete a file

Example:

```
[user1@noname00 contacts]$ rm /home/user1/letters/vocals.txt
[user1@noname00 contacts]$ ls /home/user1/letters/
[user1@noname00 contacts]$
```

Move and rename a file

Example:

- Move

  [user1@noname00 contacts]$ mv vocals.txt /home/user1/letters/
  [user1@noname00 contacts]$ ls /home/user/letters/
  vocals.txt
  [user1@noname00 contacts]$

- Rename

  [user1@noname00 contacts]$ cd ../letters/
  [user1@noname00 letters]$ mv vocals.txt vocals1.txt
  [user1@noname00 letters]$ ls -la
  total 4
  drwxrwxr-x 2 user1 user1 25 oct 27 20:01 .
  drwx------ 6 user1 user1 132 oct 27 19:57 ..
  -rw-rw-r-- 1 user1 user1 14 oct 27 19:50 vocals1.txt
  [user1@noname00 letters]$

Create a link to a file

A link allows access to the original file under another name or another route.

- Example 1:

  [user1@noname00 letters]$ ls -la
  total 4
  drwxrwxr-x 2 user1 user1 43 oct 27 20:34 .
  drwx------ 6 user1 user1 132 oct 27 19:57 ..
  -rw-rw-r-- 1 user1 user1 14 oct 27 19:50 vocals1.txt
  lrwxrwxrwx 1 user1 user1 12 oct 27 20:34 vocals.txt -> vocals1.txt
  [user1@noname00 letters]$ cat vocals.txt
  a, e, i, o, u

[user1@noname00 letters]$

> Example 2:

[user1@noname00 other_directory]$ pwd
/home/user1/other_directory
[user1@noname00 other_directory]$ ln -s ../letters/vocals1.txt vocals.txt
[user1@noname00 other_directory]$ ls -la
total 0
drwxrwxr-x 2 user1 user1 24 oct 27 20:36 .
drwx------ 7 user1 user1 154 oct 27 20:35 ..
lrwxrwxrwx 1 user1 user1 22 oct 27 20:36 vocals.txt -> ../letters/vocals.txt
[user1@noname00 other_directory]$ cat vocals.txt
a, e, i, o, u
[user1@noname00 other_directory]$

Synchronize file systems

We will use the command *rsync*. It works at follows:

rsync --delete --recursive --times -og --links --perms --hard-links\ /tmp/rsync/ root@servidor_remoto:/tmp/rsync

--delete: Removes files that exist on the target but not the origin.
--recursive: Copy directories recursively (all subdirectories).
--times: Send modification dates and times of the files.
-og: Does not change the user or group of files.
--links: Copy the links.
--perms: Copy the permissions.
--hard-links: Copy the hard-links if they are within the directory that is copying.

Find a file

The find command is responsible for this function. You can choose from a multitude of search criteria. As we said earlier, the man we facilitate the task of choosing the parameters that we need.

Below are some examples of operation:

> Example search by name:

[user1@noname00 ~]$ pwd
/home/user1
[user1@noname00 ~]$ find . -name voc*.txt -exec ls -la {} \;
-rw-rw-r-- 1 user1 user1 14 oct 27 19:50 ./letters/vocals1.txt
[user1@noname00 ~]$ cd letters/
[user1@noname00 letter]$ ll
total 4
-rw-rw-r-- 1 user1 user1 14 oct 27 19:50 vocals1.txt
[user1@noname00 letters]$

> Example search by date:

The important parameter of this type of search is called mtime and works as follows:

-mtime 0: Find files modified between now and 1 day ago, that is, in the last 24 hours.
-mtime -1: Find files modified less than 1 day ago.
-mtime 1: Find files modified between 24 and 48 hours ago.
-mtime +1: Find files modified more than 48 hours ago.
-mmin +5 -mmin -10: find files modified between 6 and 9 minutes ago.

[user1@noname00 ~]$ find . -mtime +15
./.bash_profile
./.gnome2
./.bashrc
./.mozilla
./.mozilla/extensions
./.mozilla/plugins
./.bash_logout
[user1@noname00 ~]$

> Example of search by name, files less than a day of creation or modification, and that the size does not revise other file systems mounted below the location indicated:

[user1@noname00 ~]$ find /home/user1/ -xdev -name ".v*" -mtime -1 -size +1 -exec ls -la {} \;
-rw------- 1 user1 user1 1342 oct 27 19:50 /home/user1/.viminfo
[user1@noname00 ~]$

> Example of search of a text into a file:

[user1@noname00 ~]$ find . -exec grep -l "This is a text" {} \;
./text.txt
[user1@noname00 ~]$

With "egrep" we will filter by more than one word. For example, if we want to filter all lines of a file that contains the words "loss" and "Nov", we will execute:

[user1@noname00 ~]$ egrep "loss|Nov" PingTest.log |grep -v "0%" |more
Thu **Nov** 18 01:54:00 MET 2010
3 packets transmitted, 2 packets received, 33% packet **loss**
Thu **Nov** 18 01:55:00 MET 2010

Pack and unpack an archive in tar format

There are multiple applications that can perform this function, however, *tar* is a standard that can group files or directories into one resulting file that retains the characteristics of each of the directories and files it contains.

Examples:

> Pack

[user1@noname00 letters]$ tar cvf vocals1.tar vocals1.txt
vocals1.txt
[user1@noname00 letters]$ rm vocals1.txt

```
[user1@noname00 letters]$ ls -l
total 12
-rw-rw-r-- 1 user1 user1 10240 oct 27 20:13 vocals1.tar
[user1@noname00 letters]$
```

- Unpack

```
[user1@noname00 letters]$ tar xvf vocals1.tar
vocals1.txt
[user1@noname00 letters]$ ls -l
total 16
-rw-rw-r-- 1 user1 user1 10240 oct 27 20:13 vocals1.tar
-rw-rw-r-- 1 user1 user1    14 oct 27 19:50 vocals1.txt
[user1@noname00 letters]$ cat vocals1.txt
a, e, i, o, u
[user1@noname00 letters]$
```

Compress and decompress a file

gzip is the application of excellence to compress and decompress files on UNIX systems, although there are other similar applications, such as *compress* or *zip*.

Example:

- Compress

```
[user1@noname00 letters]$ gzip vocals1.tar
[user1@noname00 letters]$ ll
total 4
-rw-rw-r-- 1 user1 user1 153 oct 27 20:13 vocals1.tar.gz
[user1@noname00 letters]$
```
- Decompress
```
[user1@noname00 letters]$ gzip -d vocals1.tar.gz
[user1@noname00 letters]$ ll
total 12
-rw-rw-r-- 1 user1 user1 10240 oct 27 20:13 vocals1.tar
```

[user1@noname00 letters]$

Depending on the version of *tar* that we have, we can use it for decompressing the *gzip* and *tar* file at once:

[user1@noname00 letters]$ tar xvzf vocals1.tar.gz
vocals1.txt
[user1@noname00 letters]$ ll
total 8
-rw-rw-r-- 1 user1 user1 153 oct 27 20:13 vocals1.tar.gz
-rw-rw-r-- 1 user1 user1 14 oct 27 19:50 vocals1.txt
[user1@noname00 letters]$

Knowing the available space in the current directory

To know if we can copy, move or save a file in a directory, it is necessary to know if we have space available for it. We found out with the command *df [directory]*.

Sample usage of the command with the current directory:

[user1@noname00 ~]$ pwd
/home/user1
[user1@noname00 ~]$ df .
S.files   Blocks 1K   Usaded   Disp Use% Mounted in
/dev/mapper/vg00-lvhome
             12277760   804860   11472900   7% /home
[user1@noname00 ~]$

[user1@noname00 ~]$ df -h /var
S.files   Blocks 1K   Usaded   Disp Use% Mounted in
/dev/mapper/vg00-lvvar
             12G   317M   12G   3% /var
[user1@noname00 ~]$

Find out which files and directories are larger

There are several ways to know this information:

Examples:

- How large is each directory?

    [root@noname00 ~]# du -k .
    8   ./.nautilus/metafiles
    24   ./.nautilus
    28   ./.VirtualBox
    4   ./vmware
    692   ./.gstreamer-0.10
    4   ./Videos
    8   ./.macromedia/Flash_Player/macromedia.com/support/flashplayer/sys/#es.mg40.mail.yahoo.com
    16   ./.macromedia/Flash_Player/macromedia.com/support/flashplayer/sys
    20   ./.macromedia/Flash_Player/macromedia.com/support/flashplayer
    24   ./.macromedia/Flash_Player/macromedia.com/support
    28   ./.macromedia/Flash_Player/macromedia.com

- How big is the set of subdirectories?

    [root@noname00 ~]# du -ks
    119416   .
    [root@noname00 ~]#

- What are the 10 largest files?

    [root@noname00 ~]# find . -exec ls -la {} \; |sort -rnk5 |head -10
    -rw-r--r-- 1 root root 17725318 sep 27 20:30 ./scripts/backup_total2008-09-27.log
    -rw-r--r-- 1 root root 17725318 sep 27 20:30 backup_total2008-09-27.log
    -rw-r--r-- 1 root root 15212544 sep 29 23:07 urlclassifier3.sqlite
    -rw-r--r-- 1 root root 15212544 sep 29 23:07 ./.mozilla/firefox/hj9hcofv.default/urlclassifier3.sqlite

```
-rw------- 1 root root 4096008 ago 27 09:36 ./.wapi/shared_fileshare-noname00-Linux-x86_64-40-11-0
-rw------- 1 root root 4096008 ago 27 09:36 shared_fileshare-noname00-Linux-x86_64-40-11-0
-rw-r--r-- 1 root root 2037926 ago 27 09:14 XPC.mfasl
-rw-r--r-- 1 root root 2037926 ago 27 09:14 ./.mozilla/firefox/hj9hcofv.default/XPC.mfasl
-rw-r--r-- 1 root root 1446620 oct  1 19:30 ./scripts/backup_total2008-10-01.log.gz
-rw-r--r-- 1 root root 1446620 oct  1 19:30 backup_total2008-10-01.log.gz
[root@noname00 ~]#
```

Know what processes are using a file system

One of the peculiarities of UNIX systems is that the space of a file will be in use until the system process that is using it does not end, even if the file is erased. In the case that we see the space of a file system is declining and we do not know the reason, might be because some application has opened a file, it is writing in it, someone has deleted by mistake, but the application has not released its space because it has not ended. This may well be an effect that causes unavailability of a system or an application, and need to know what processes are using the file system is affected to be able to end its execution and release the space. This is done as follows:

Example:

> In a session, we open a text file:

[user1@noname00 ~]$ vi test.txt

> We opened another session and review what processes are using the file:
[user1@noname00 ~]$ /sbin/fuser /home/user1
/home/user1:   5694c 10469c 10612c
[user1@noname00 ~]$ ps -ef |grep 10612
user1 **10612** 5694 0 21:13 pts/0   00:00:00 **vi test.txt**

We know that the process, whose system identifier is 10612, match to *vi* process opened on the first session.

There is another more complete command which, among other things, also includes this feature. It's called *lsof*:

```
[user1@noname00 ~]$ /usr/sbin/lsof /home/user1
COMMAND  PID    USER  FD   TYPE DEVICE SIZE  NODE NAME
bash     5694  user1  cwd  DIR  253,4  4096  25138 /home/user1
bash    10469  user1  cwd  DIR  253,4  4096  25138 /home/user1
vi      10612  user1  cwd  DIR  253,4  4096  25138 /home/user1
lsof    10662  user1  cwd  DIR  253,4  4096  25138 /home/user1
lsof    10663  user1  cwd  DIR  253,4  4096  25138 /home/user1
[user1@noname00 ~]$
```

Knowing what type is a file

There are different types of file, text, binary, or any specific application. The command to find out this information is called *file*.

> Example:
>
> > [user1@noname00 myfiles]$ file myfile.txt
> > myfile.txt: ASCII text
> > [user1@noname00 myfiles]$

Translate to text a binary file

The command *strings* writes to display all those text characters in a binary file. For example, LVM (later will explain what it is) keeps the configuration of the disks that are used every VG in a binary file is not legible to the naked eye, however, *strings* we will show the information from the disks used:

```
[noname00] root:/root # strings /etc/lvmtab
/dev/vg00
/dev/dsk/c1t2d0
/dev/dsk/c2t0d0
/dev/dsk/c1t0d0
/dev/dsk/c2t2d0
```

Run an application using the graphical mode

In the following example we use the command *xclock*, which opens a window with a clock in graphical mode.

- We try to run the application *xclock* unsuccessfully for lack of graphical environment with our user:

    ```
    [root@noname00 ~]# su - user1
    [user1@noname00 ~]$ xclock
    No protocol specified
    Error: Can't open display: :0.0
    [user1@noname00 ~]$
    ```

- Load the environment variable *DISPLAY* to export the screen to our terminal and, thus, be able to run *xclock*:

    ```
    [user1@noname00 ~]$ exit
    logout
    [root@noname00 ~]# xhost +
    access control disabled, clients can connect from any host
    [root@noname00 ~]#
    [root@noname00 ~]# su - user1
    [user1@noname00 ~]$ export DISPLAY=:0.0
    [user1@noname00 ~]$ xclock
    ```

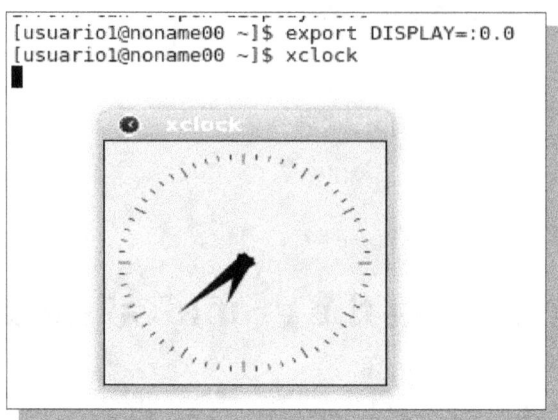

In the example above, we have authorized that any client can run a graphical application remotely, using the command "xhost +", however, this may be a security hole in our system. The creators of graphic environments, introduced two authorization systems in order to run graphical applications from a remote system. These systems are called *xhost* and *xauth*.

xhost

Allows to load a graphics application if the IP we are connecting to server is among those authorized, if it is, we can load a graphical application remotely, otherwise the connection is closed.

This system is not too sure, because in NAT connections will have more than one user using the same IP.

Examples:

- xhost +user1: Adds the host user "user1" to the list of authorized IPs.
- xhost -user1: Disable the authorization of the host user "user1".
- xhost+: Disables authorization control and all clients can connect
- xhost -: Enables de xhost control.

XAuth

This system is more secure than above, because allows to connects those clients who know a secret identifier that the server keeps in memory. This identifier is called MIT-MAGIC-COOKIE.

Next, is shown an example which adds the authorization of the MAGIC-COOKIE of another system user to our user:

- We login to the system with the user we want to authorize.
- We show his COOKIE.

> xauth list → "secaiasp01/unix:10   MIT-MAGIC-COOKIE-1 966985c2dcfefbc583cb745012c584b2"
> set | grep DISPL → "DISPLAY=localhost:10.0"

- We change to the authorizer user, for example, user1 (su – user1).
- We add the authorization:

> [user1@noname00 ~]$ xauth add secaiasp01/unix:10 MIT-MAGIC-COOKIE-1 966985c2dcfefbc583cb745012c584b2
> [user1@noname00 ~]$ export DISPLAY=localhost:10.0

Basic commands related to the processes

A process is a job that is running on the operating system together with the structure that is created for the program to access the hardware resources such as CPU, memory and input and output devices (I / O).

In UNIX systems, the kernel, or core of the operating system stores information for effective operation:

- Process identifiers, user and group owner who implemented it.
- Environment variables, current directory, libraries that are needed...
- Input and output information (data to be read or write on a hard disk, for example).

- State of the process (running, idle, defunct ...).
- Memory addresses of the process.

A process can run several times at the same time or many different processes can be running at once. For example, two users of the system could successfully launch the command *find* at once, while another user executes the command *vi*, and each would get the result they expected. This is called multitasking. The operating system is responsible for managing the CPU time to each of the processes in order to minimize the waiting time for each of them and appear to have been running at the same on servers with more than one core or more than one processor, multitasking is more efficient to be able to execute the various processes in different CPUs, that is, it is possible that two processes are really running at the same time, instead of going to share the same CPU in very small fractions of time as in systems with a single core (a processor can have more than one core).

Process ID o PID: The system shows a unique identifier to each process.

Parent Process ID o PPID: A process of UNIX is created invoking the fork function of the operating system, which creates an identical copy of the process that invoked, except that the new PID has a different, the PPID of the new process is the PID of the original process and creating a structure of consumption of CPU, memory, etc.. for the new process. The PPID is the father of the PID.

User ID o UID: It is for the user's operating system that launched the process.

Effective user ID EEUID: Indicates whether the process has permission to access files and other system resources.

GID y EGID: They do the same functions as ID and EEUID but for groups of users.

A *zombie* or *defunct* process is one that has completed its execution but still has an entry in the process table, allowing to the process that has created read the status of its exit. As a general rule, these processes do not cause damage to the system, but can always be some exceptions.

The following are some of the commands of system related with the processes:

Knowing the processes that are running on the system

Is used the command *ps*.

Knowing all system processes that are running:

    ps -e
    ps -ef
    ps -eF
    ps -ely

View the tree of processes:

    ps -ejH
    ps axjf

Choose the columns we want to see:

    ps -eo pid,tid,class,rtprio,ni,pri,psr,pcpu,stat,wchan:14,comm
    ps axo stat,euid,ruid,tty,tpgid,sess,pgrp,ppid,pid,pcpu,comm
    ps -eopid,tt,user,fname,tmout,f,wchan

Example:

```
[user1@noname00 ~]$ ps -fU root |more
UID        PID  PPID  C STIME     TTY  TIME      CMD
root       1    0     0 18:07     ?    00:00:00  /sbin/init
root       2    0     0 18:07     ?    00:00:00  [kthreadd]
root       3    2     0 18:07     ?    00:00:00  [migration/0]
root       4    2     0 18:07     ?    00:00:00  [ksoftirqd/0]
root       5    2     0 18:07     ?    00:00:00  [watchdog/0]
root       6    2     0 18:07     ?    00:00:00  [migration/1]
```

```
usuario1@noname00 ~]$ ps -flU usuario1
S UID        PID  PPID C PRI  NI ADDR SZ WCHAN  STIME TTY          TIME CMD
S usuario1  4728  4727 0  80   0 -  22724 read_c 06:48 pts/0    00:00:00 -bash
S usuario1  4962  4961 0  80   0 -  22179 wait   07:20 pts/1    00:00:00 -bash
R usuario1  5556  4962 0  80   0 -  22135 -      07:28 pts/1    00:00:00 ps -flU usuario1
usuario1@noname00 ~]$
```

The most important characteristics that need to know about the processes are:

> UID → Owner of the process.
> PID → ID of the process.
> PPID → ID of the parent process.
> C → Amount of CPU resources that the process has been used recently. The *kernel* (core operating system) uses this information to establish the priority.
> PRI → Priority of the process.
> NI → nice value. A positive value indicates less CPU time.
> STIME → Time to start the process.
> TTY → Terminal associated with the process.
> TIME → CPU time associated with the process.
> CMD → Command executed.

Reviewing the consumption of CPU and memory each process

The top command is responsible for the show with regularity, a report of the processes that are running on the system and ordered by CPU consumption. This command is very useful to know which of them could be causing delays in the system.

It also shows statistics of the consumption of system memory and each process, as shown in the following screen shot.

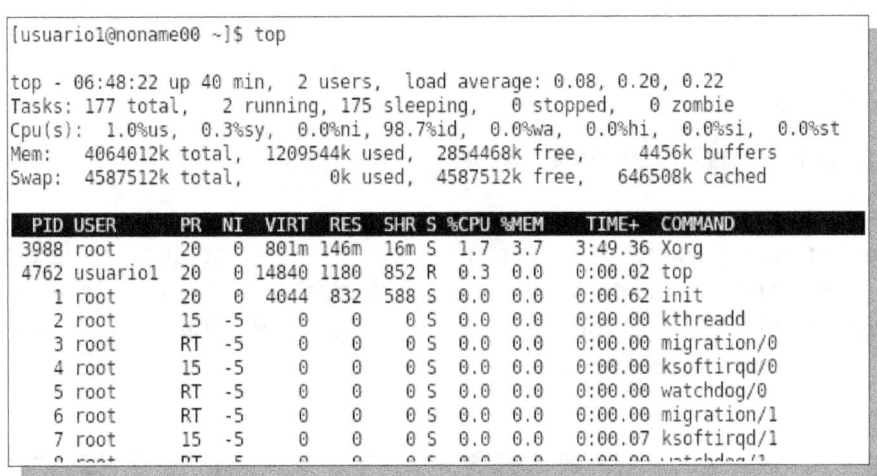

If we want to know what processes consume more memory, the next instruction will order it, from highest to lowest, and its consumption in KB:

[user1@noname00 ~]$ UNIX95= ps -e -o vsz=Kbytes -o ruser -o pid,args=Command-Line | sort -rnk1 | more
811436 David   4643 /usr/lib64/openoffice.org/program/swriter.bin -writer
538452 root   3522 /usr/lib/vmware/webAccess/java/jre1.5.0_15/bin/webAccess -client -Xmx64m -XX:MinHeapFreeRatio=30 -XX:MaxHeapFreeRatio=30 -Djava.util.logging.manager=org.apach e.juli.ClassLoaderLogManager -Djava.endorsed.dirs=/usr/lib/vmware/webAccess/tomcat/apache-tomcat-6.0.16/common/endorsed -classpath /usr/lib/vmware/webAccess/tomcat/apache-tomcat-6.0.16/bin/bootstrap.jar:/usr/lib/vmware/webAccess/tomcat/apache-tomcat-6.0.16/bin/commons-logging-api.jar -Dcatalina.base=/usr/lib/vmware/webAccess/tomcat/apache-tomcat-6.0.16 -Dcatalina.home=/usr/lib/vmware/webAccess/tomcat/apache-tomcat-6.0.16 -Djava.io.tmpdir=/usr/lib/vmware/webAccess/tomcat/apache-tomcat-6.0.16/temp org.apache.catalina.startup.Bootstrap s
tart
502896 David   4186 nautilus --no-default-window --sm-client-id default3
411172 David   4155 /usr/libexec/gnome-settings-daemon
365304 David   4660 gnome-terminal
346604 David   4262 /usr/libexec/clock-applet --oaf-activate-

iid=OAFIID:GNOME_ClockApplet_Factory –oaf-ior-fd=29

Forcing the completion of a process

We will kill a process when we detect an anomaly in its operation or is causing any impact on the system. The command that performs this function is to kill and is responsible for sending a signal to a process such as *SIGKILL*. Some of more interesting signals are the following:

Number of signal	Name	Function
0	Exit to the shell	Occurs after the execution of a script
1	SIGHUP	It was sent to all processes associated with a terminal when it finishes its connection. Its action is the completion of all proceedings of the meeting.
2	SIGINT	Is sent when you press the key combination *Control-C* (break).
3	SIGQUIT	Leave a dump to be analyzed (*Control-4*).
4	SIGILL	Sent when the hardware detects an illegal instruction. Its action is to complete the process and generate a dump.
6	SIGIOT	Hardware failure.
8	SIGFPE	Floating-point error.
9	SIGKILL	Force the completion of the process.
10	SIGBUS	It occurs when a process tries to access an area of faulty memory.
11	SIGSEGV	Violation memory segment.
13	SIGPIPE	Attempt to write in a pipeline in

		which no one reads.
14	SIGALARM	Is sent to a process where some of its timer reaches 0.
15	SIGTERM	Indicates a process that must end its implementation in an orderly. Can be ignored.
16, 17	SIGUSR1, SIGUSR2	Reserved for the user.
18	SIGCLD	Is sent to the father of a process if it dies.
19	SIGPWR	Power failure

With the *-l* argument we will see all the signs that can be sent to a process.

Example:

> We opened a session and run the command *vi*, that then we will kill.

    [user1@noname00 ~]$ vi myfile.txt

> We open another meeting and we look for the PID of *vi*

    [user1@noname00 ~]$ ps -U user1
      PID TTY   TIME CMD
     4728 pts/0   00:00:00 bash
     4962 pts/1   00:00:00 bash
     4997 pts/0   00:00:00 vi
     5000 pts/1   00:00:00 ps
    [user1@noname00 ~]$

> We kill the process by sending the signal 9 to its PID:

    [user1@noname00 ~]$ kill -9 4997
    [user1@noname00 ~]$

> We come to the session where we had executed the command, and we find the

following message:
    killed
    [user1@noname00 ~]$

Capture the signal of completion of a process

It is useful to know whether the process has finished anomalous.

Example:

    [user1@noname00 scripts]$ ./trap.sh
    Collector of signals:
    ^CSIGINT received signal

The message *SIGINT received signal* what we see when we press Control-C (Signal 2).

The source code of the program is:

    [user1@noname00 scripts]$ cat trap.sh
    #!/bin/sh

    [user1@noname00 scripts]$ cat trap.sh
    #!/bin/sh

    echo Collector of signals:
    trap 'echo SIGNINT signal received' 2;

    while true
    do

        :

    done
    [user1@noname00 scripts]$

Modify the priority of execution of a process

The priority of CPU usage of a process is evaluated from 1 to 19, being the 19th most penalized. By default, a process has priority 10 when run, but we can launch it with a different priority through the *nice* command.

Example:

    nice -8 Name_of_the_program &

    [user1@noname00 ~]$ nice -8 vi

Look at the column NI of the *vi* process:

```
[user1@noname00 ~]$ ps -flU user1
F S UID         PID  PPID C PRI  NI ADDR SZ WCHAN   STIME TTY       TIME CMD
4 S user1  5083  5082 0 80   0 - 22179 wait    11:45 pts/1    00:00:00 -bash
0 R user1  5118  5083 0 80   0 - 22134 -       11:45 pts/1    00:00:00 ps -f
[user1@noname00 ~]$
```

Once launched the process, with the *root* user, we can change its priority through the command *renice*. Example:

    [root@noname00 ~]# renice -n 20 20699
    20699: old priority 4, new priority 20

    [root@noname00 ~]#

Knowing the time of execution of a process

time executes the command that is passed as an argument and, at the end, get real-time statistics that has been taken to run (real), the CPU time of (user) and the CPU time that the system has been used to run (sys)

Example:

>[user1@noname00 ~]$ time ls
>contacts letters nohup.out other_directory scripts
>
>real   0m0.024s
>user   0m0.000s
>sys   0m0.003s
>[user1@noname00 ~]$

Running processes in background

The background process those that release the shell to allow us to launch other jobs while the is still running.

To run a background process, we shall follow the syntax *Process_Name &*.

Example:

>[user1@noname00 ~]$ ls > test.txt &
>[1] 8788
>[user1@noname00 ~]$ ps -ef |grep 8788
>user1 8790 8754 2 10:05 pts/0   00:00:00 grep 8788
>[1]+ Done   ls --color=auto > test.txt
>[user1@noname00 ~]$ cat test.txt
>contacts
>letters
>other_directory
>test.txt
>[user1@noname00 ~]$

While the command *ls > test.txt &* was in progress the shell was released to run *ps -ef | grep 8788*, although we could have executed any other process that we would have liked. With *cat*, we see that the above process has completed successfully, as it shows the result we expected.

There is another command called *nohup* which also serves to launch processes in the background but with the difference that, although our session finishes, the process will remain until the end. The priority of the process is increased to 5. It is very useful for launching heavy work or who will take a long time.

Example:

    [user1@noname00 ~]$ nohup ls -l > test.txt &
    [1] 8796

The file *nohup.out* is responsible for collecting information on the process launched by *nohup*. It is your standard output.

Planning tasks with cron

All UNIX systems have a task scheduler called *cron* which is responsible for launching a process at the moment we have indicated in its configuration file. Normally files planning tasks are stored in */var/spool/cron/username*, but it is not necessary to go up there to be able to edit the file. For this is the command crontab.

Task Scheduler is very useful to run jobs at times when we can not stand in front of the screen or when we do not know the exact time at which to finish a process to be able to launch another that requires the completion of the first (to this it is called batch). To see it more clearly, imagine that during the day there is a department of Call Center that is using an application. This, in turn, needs to connect to a database whose backup is planned so offline, that is, you need to stop the database to make a backup. In this case, we would need to run the stop at a time when no one using the application, so we could schedule a job that will run from early morning to stop the database, make a copy and start the BD when the previous step is ready.

An example of planning:

    ➤ We edit the cron file:

        [user1@noname00 ~]$ crontab -e

> We enter the following lines:

    30 4 * * * my_backup.sh > */dev/null 2>&1*

The command "> /dev/null 2>&1" indicates that script as programs that invokes forwards the output to /dev/null.

What we do is run every day at 4:30 my_backup.sh job. Crontab follows the syntax:

    minute hour day months days_of_the_week command

If we want to run a command from one to five minutes of each hour, the syntax would be:

    1-5 * * * * my_backup.sh > */dev/null 2>&1*

If we also want to run only on Saturday and Sunday, we will write:

    1-5 * * * 6,0 my_backup.sh > */dev/null 2>&1*

being 6 on Saturday and 0 on Sunday. This may vary depending on your operating system. For sure, is best to revise the help of the command through *man crontab*.

If the script configured is not redirected to any log, we must send its output to *"> /dev/null 2>&1"*, as is shown in the examples above, otherwise the mail messages queue will be fill.

Other crontab parameters:

    crontab [-ledc] [file]

    crontab file → Specify the configuration file.
    -l → We see the tasks that we have planned.
    -e → We edit the planning tasks.
    -d → We delete the planning file.
    -c dir → Define the directory of crontabs.

The files */etc/cron.deny* and *cron.allow* serve to allow or deny the use of crontab to some users. They are used as follows:

```
[root@noname00 etc]# cat /etc/cron.deny
daemon
bin
nuucp
listen
nobody
noaccess
[root@noname00 etc]#
```

Reviewing the processes that are running users connected

Example:

```
[user1@noname00 ~]$ w
 19:11:30 up  2:12,  5 users,  load average: 1,92, 2,46, 2,98
USER     TTY      FROM             LOGIN@   IDLE  JCPU  PCPU WHAT
user1    tty7     :0               17:00    0.00s 15:19 0.12s gnome-session
user1    pts/0    :0.0             17:28    10:01 5:24  2:04 gnome-terminal
user1    pts/1    :0.0             19:06    3:42  0.01s 0.01s bash
user1    pts/3    :0.0             18:46    0.00s 0.02s 2:04 gnome-terminal
user1    pts/4    :0.0             19:05    2:35  0.02s 2:04 gnome-terminal
[user1@noname00 ~]$
```

Basic commands related to the filters

If we look at some of the examples we have been seeing until now, have been used commands like *grep* or *sort* through a pipe (|). The objective was to obtain a partial result of the first command, only those data that concern us, or take out an orderly outcome. This is achieved through the use of filters. There are different types and functions:

Search for text strings

grep is responsible for this task.

Examples:

We will use the file *names.txt* to teach various uses of *grep*:

>   [user1@noname00 ~]$ cat names.txt
>   David
>   Raquel
>   Silvia
>   Javi
>   Alberto
>   [user1@noname00 ~]$

- We want to know if there is the name Javi:

>   [user1@noname00 ~]$ grep Javi names.txt
>   Javi
>   [user1@noname00 ~]$

    The result has been the word Javi, which is what we were looking for, however, we have written the word exactly as it was included in the file but, and if we had written in capital letters?

>   [user1@noname00 ~]$ grep JAVI names.txt
>   [user1@noname00 ~]$

    We would not have found anything.

- The following example will ignore the upper or lower case letters:

>   [user1@noname00 ~]$ grep -i jAVi names.txt
>   Javi
>   [user1@noname00 ~]$

- And in what line number is the word Javi?

    [user1@noname00 ~]$ grep -n Jav names.txt
    4:Javi
    [user1@noname00 ~]$

- Now we are interested to know all the names of the file, the least of Javi. To do this we use a parameter of exclusion:

    [user1@noname00 ~]$ grep -v Javi namess.txt
    David
    Raquel
    Silvia
    Alberto
    [user1@noname00 ~]$

    It also could have used *-i* next to *-v*:

    [user1@noname00 ~]$ grep -iv JAVi names.txt
    David
    Raquel
    Silvia
    Alberto
    [user1@noname00 ~]$

- *grep* can also be used with a pipe, that is, we can filter the text of a command output.

    [user1@noname00 ~]$ ls -la | grep -i Names
    -rw-rw-r-- 1 user1 user1   32 nov 2 08:59 names.txt
    [user1@noname00 ~]$

- Finally, we show how to skip blank lines from a text file:

    grep -v "^$" archivo.txt > archivo_nuevo.txt

As always, remember that the help of the command by *man* may contain other parameters in line with our needs.

Sort strings

sort is the instruction that is used to format the output of a command in an orderly manner (alphabetically, numerically, by dates ...).

Examples:

> We ordered the file *names.txt* alphabetically:

```
[user1@noname00 ~]$ sort -d names.txt
Alberto
David
Javi
Raquel
Silvia
[user1@noname00 ~]$
```

> We order from highest to lowest, the files by their size:

```
[user1@noname00 ~]$ ls -la |sort -rnk5 -f
-rw------- 1 user1 user1 12288 oct 29 07:20 .file.txt.swp
-rw------- 1 user1 user1  5516 nov  2 09:41 .viminfo
-rw------- 1 user1 user1  5386 nov  1 10:09 .bash_history
drwx------ 5 user1 user1  4096 nov  2 09:41 .
-rw-r--r-- 1 user1 user1   176 feb 29  2008 .bash_profile
-rw-r--r-- 1 user1 user1   124 feb 29  2008 .bashrc
drwxr-xr-x 6 root  root     61 oct 27 19:29 ..
-rw------- 1 user1 user1    52 oct 31 19:01 .lesshst
drwxr-xr-x 4 user1 user1    37 may 30 22:17 .mozilla
-rw-rw-r-- 1 user1 user1    33 nov  2 09:41 names.txt
drwxrwxr-x 2 user1 user1    20 oct 31 18:49 scripts
-rw-r--r-- 1 user1 user1    18 feb 29  2008 .bash_logout
drwxr-xr-x 2 user1 user1     6 abr  6  2008 .gnome2
total 52
-rw-rw-r-- 1 user1 user1     0 oct 29 10:13 nohup.out
```

[user1@noname00 ~]$

The parameters used in the above example are:

r → Reverse order.
n → Numerical order.
k5 → Column 5 of the output of *ls -la* is that it has ordered.

If we do not want to see the files containing the word *bash*, we could have supplemented this command, with *grep* through a pipe:

```
[user1@noname00 ~]$ ls -la |grep -v bash| sort -rnk5 -f
-rw------- 1 user1 user1 12288 oct 29 07:20 .file.txt.swp
-rw------- 1 user1 user1  5516 nov  2 09:41 .viminfo
drwx------ 5 user1 user1  4096 nov  2 09:41 .
drwxr-xr-x 6 root  root     61 oct 27 19:29 ..
-rw------- 1 user1 user1    52 oct 31 19:01 .lesshst
drwxr-xr-x 4 user1 user1    37 may 30 22:17 .mozilla
-rw-rw-r-- 1 user1 user1    33 nov  2 09:41 names.txt
drwxrwxr-x 2 user1 user1    20 oct 31 18:49 scripts
drwxr-xr-x 2 user1 user1     6 abr  6 2008 .gnome2
total 52
-rw-rw-r-- 1 user1 user1     0 oct 29 10:13 nohup.out
[user1@noname00 ~]$
```

Remove the repeated lines of a text

uniq removes all fields repeated least one (the first).

Example:

> In the end file *names.txt* we add the name *David* in order to have doubled:

```
[user1@noname00 ~]$ cat names.txt
David
Raquel
Silvia
```

    Javi
    Alberto
    David
    [user1@noname00 ~]$

- We order the file by removing the elements repeated and, besides, we want to know how many times an item has been found:

        [user1@noname00 ~]$ cat names.txt |sort -d |uniq -c
        1 Alberto
        2 David
        1 Javi
        1 Raquel
        1 Silvia
        [user1@noname00 ~]$

Lines, words and characters counter

The command *wc* done this and other functions:

Examples:

- We count the number of lines of the file *names.txt*:

        [user1@noname00 ~]$ wc -l names.txt
        5 names.txt
        [user1@noname00 ~]$

- We count the number of words that has the same file:

        [user1@noname00 ~]$ wc -w names.txt
        5 names.txt
        [user1@noname00 ~]$

- We count the number of files we have in the current directory:

        [user1@noname00 ~]$ ls -la |wc -l

15
[user1@noname00 ~]$

Cut characters from a text string

Sometimes, the output of a command gives us too much information and only need to know a value or a field of all this data gives us. To filter the desired values, we can use *cut*.

Examples:

- We have the file *fields.txt* in which separates each field with the symbol ":":

    [user1@noname00 ~]$ cat fields.txt
    field1:field2:field3:field4
    c1v1 :c1v2 :c1v3 :c1v4
    c2v1 :c2v2 :c2v3 :c2v4
    [user1@noname00 ~]$

- We want to view the fields 2 and 4:

    [user1@noname00 ~]$ cut -d ':' -f 2,4 fields.txt
    field2:field4
    c1v2 :c1v4
    c2v2 :c2v4
    [user1@noname00 ~]$

    With the parameter *-d* we have indicated that the character that separates the fields is ":" and with *-f* are the areas we want to see.

- Now we have another file with the alphabet and want to see the letters in the 4 to 14:

    [user1@noname00 ~]$ cut -c 4-14 alphabet.txt
    defghijklmn
    [user1@noname00 ~]$

Replace a string by another

The syntax of the command *sed* is as follows:

sed 's/original_string/new_string/' File_name

Example:

>[user1@noname00 ~]$ sed 's/Silvia/Laura/' names.txt
>David
>Raquel
>Laura
>Javi
>Alberto
>David
>[user1@noname00 ~]$

See the first few lines of text

With *head* we will see the number of lines indicated, beginning with the start of a file or a command if we have used through a pipe.

Examples:

>[user1@noname00 ~]$ head -2 names.txt
>David
>Raquel
>[user1@noname00 ~]$
>
>
>[user1@noname00 ~]$ ls -la |head -6
>total 68
>drwx------ 5 user1 user1 4096 nov 2 12:32 .
>drwxr-xr-x 6 root   root   61 oct 27 19:29 ..
>-rw-rw-r-- 1 user1 user1   23 nov 2 10:37 alphabet.txt
>-rw------- 1 user1 user1 7115 nov 2 12:32 .bash_history

```
-rw-r--r-- 1 user1 user1    18 feb 29  2008 .bash_logout
[user1@noname00 ~]$
```

See the last lines of a text

tail acts like *head* but instead of showing the first few lines of text, displays the latest.

Compare the contents of two text files

With diff can know if two files are exactly the same text or there is any difference between them.

Example:

- We copy the file *names.txt* to *names2.txt* and in each of the files we add a different name at the end. Both files would be as follows:

    ```
    [user1@noname00 ~]$ cat names.txt
    David
    Raquel
    Silvia
    Javi
    Alberto
    Marcos

    [user1@noname00 ~]$ cat names2.txt
    David
    Raquel
    Silvia
    Javi
    Alberto
    Pepe
    [user1@noname00 ~]$
    ```

- We review the differences between the two files:

```
[user1@noname00 ~]$ diff names.txt names2.txt
6c6
< Marcos
---
> Pepe
[user1@noname00 ~]$
```

It was detected that the line number six is different.

The command *comm* also compares two files:

```
[user1@noname00 ~]$ comm names.txt names2.txt
		David
		Raquel
		Silvia
		Javi
		Alberto
Marcos
	Pepe
[user1@noname00 ~]$
```

Part 2

UNIX administration knowledges

Administration of UNIX systems

Introduction

All the knowledge we have gained so far are focused on a user does not need to know how it runs a UNIX system. A systems administrator is responsible for installing the operating system, create users, groups, security policies, configuring network interfaces, apply for permits for access to ports to the administrators of communications, resizing file systems, printers configurations, giving accounts of FTP and SFTP, server maintenance, high availability configurations and contingency, revision of hardware failures and crashes, software installation, support to the users and developers, performance system review and much more things.

All this is what we will see from now on.

What happens during the boot of the operating system?

A systems administrator must know the stages of starting a UNIX system in order to resolve or intuit the reason for any impact that occurs during this phase or to customize the way they are starts and stops the system. The first thing that happens during startup, is the verification of the proper functioning of the hardware. If all is well, will read the boot sector to load the operating system kernel in memory.

He then proceeded to load the operating system and run the init to initialize the processes set in the inittab file (if we use a system derived from System V), how to boot the system into multi user mode, mount file systems, set the hostname, start services... to finally be able to access the console or open a connection to local or remote system.

Usually inittab we will be found in the directory /etc.

inittab and runlevels

The operating system can boot in different states. This is called runlevel and may be different depending on the type of UNIX system that we are using. For example, runlevels of of an HP-UX may be different in a Solaris and a RedHat.

Example:

Runlevels of a RedHat	
Runlevel	**Description**
0	Stop
1	Single user
2	Multi user mode without NFS (Network File system)
3	Multi user full mode
4	Not used
5	Graphic mode (X11)
6	Restart

Runlevels of a Solaris	
Runlevel	**Description**
0	PROM mode. It is used to shut down or to perform any function in PROM mode (hardware maintenance).
S	Single user. Mounting the minimum number of file systems and minimal services.
1	Single user mode administrative. All file systems are mounted and minimal services.
2	Single user mode without network services.
3	All services are started.
4	Reserved for the administrator system.
5	Firmware state. There is only access from console.
6	Operating system stopped.

Runlevels supported by our operating system often described and commented in the *inittab* file:

```
# Default runlevel. The runlevels used are:
# 0 - halt (Do NOT set initdefault to this)
# 1 - Single user mode
# 2 - Multiuser, without NFS (The same as 3, if you do not have networking)
# 3 - Full multiuser mode
# 4 - unused
# 5 - X11
# 6 - reboot (Do NOT set initdefault to this)
```

To know at what runlevel has booted the system, simply type in any of the following commands:

```
[root@noname00 ~]# runlevel
N 5
[root@noname00 ~]#
[root@noname00 ~]# who -r
```

```
`run-level' 5 2008-11-03 07:18
[root@noname00 ~]#
```

If we want to change the runlevel, we will type the number *init number_of_runlevel* with the root user. In production environments, this should never be done during the hours in which the service is provided, otherwise, the users could be damaged because of the stop working of the applications that are running on the server.

If we look at the configuration of *inittab*, we will see that, depending on the runlevel to boot the system, are called some scripts or others. These programs are located in the directories /etc/rc*. Scripts beginning with "S" are run at boot (start), while those that start with "K", are executed during the shutdown (kill).

inittab syntax is as follows:

    id:level:action:processes

- **id** → It is a unique sequence of one to four characters that identifies an entry in this file.
- **level** → Corresponds to the runlevel.
- **action** → Tells how to run the process outlined in the next field. There are different types of action:
    - **respawn:** Start the process if it is not running. If the process dies, is restarted. It continues with the next line of inittab before the end of the boot of the current process.
    - **wait:** The process is started and is expected to complete the boot before continuing with the next line.
    - **boot:** The process is run during boot. If it dies, is not rebooted. *init* continues with the next line, although the process has not yet finished boot.
    - **bootwait:** Same as above except that it is expected that the process has completed its boot.
    - **powerfail:** It runs on receiving the signal of power failure.
    - **powerwait:** Same as above but is expected that the process has completed its boot.
    - **off:** If the process is running, *init* will send a signal to end its execution

and will kill if it still continues after twenty seconds.
- **initdefault:** This indicates the default runlevel.

Users and groups administration

Concepts

The *root* user exists on all UNIX systems and has privileges to do anything in the operating system. It is the system administrator. For that reason, his password must be complicated and will have to activate all the security mechanisms to protect this account, otherwise our system would be vulnerable to an attack and we could be victims of information theft or loss of data. His UID is always 0:

```
[root@noname00 ~]# id
uid=0(root) gid=0(root)
groups=0(root),1(bin),2(daemon),3(sys),4(adm),6(disk),10(wheel)
[root@noname00 ~]
```

In UNIX systems, each file or directory has permissions for reading, writing and execution for the user, group that belongs, and the other users. In this way, we avoid that any user can modify, execute or read any information that should not have access. To identify the permissions of a file, simply type the command *ls -l* file, as shown below:

```
[user1@noname00 scripts]$ ls -l script.sh
-rwxr-x--- 1 user1 user1 7 nov  3 16:10 script.sh
[user1@noname00 scripts]$
```

Looking at the first field that shows the command output, we find that the user owns the file has the privilege of reading, writing and execution, the group can read and run the script, and other users can not do anything with this file. In addition, we see that the owner of the file is the user *user1* and the group has the same name. All of this information we see as follows:

➢ The value of the first field is: -rwxr-x---

- From left to right, the second, third and fourth character (rwx) indicate privileges for the user owns the file.
- The following three characters (r-x) are the permissions allocated to the group the file.
- And the last three (---) refer to the permissions of other users.
- The privilege "r" means is are allowed to read the file.
- The privilege "w" allows the writing of it.
- The "x" allows run.
- A minus ("-") shows a lack of permits.
- The first "user1" is the system user owns the file.
- The second "user1" is the system that belongs to the file.

We still need to know what the first character ("-"). If instead of the symbol "minus" we saw the letter *d*, would indicate that it is a directory and if we saw the letter *l*, would know that this is a link to another file or directory. A minus means that a file is ordinary.

Add a group to the system

groupadd (or *addgroup* in other systems) is the command for this function. With the *-g* argument we assign manually a group identifier, which must be unique.

Example:

    [root@noname00 /]# groupadd -g 601 user1
    [root@noname00 /]#

When we get the prompt of the system, we will have added the group and the information will be reflected in the file */etc/group*:

    [root@noname00 /]# grep user1 /etc/group
    user1:x:601:
    [root@noname00 /]#

Create an user account

useradd (or *adduser* on some systems) will add new users.

Example:

>[root@noname00 /]# useradd -c "Mi first user" -d /home/user1 -g 601 -u 601 user1

The parameters used in the example above serve to:

> -c → Add a comment or description to the user.
> -d → Specify the working directory of the new account.
> -g → It assigns the group to which the user belongs.
> -u → It assigns a unique identifier.
> user1 → Is the name of the account.

We verify that the information has saved correctly in the file *passwd:*

>[root@noname00 /]# cat /etc/passwd |grep user1
>user1:x:601:601:Mi first user:/home/user1:/bin/bash
>[root@noname00 /]#

According to the encryption system that we are using the encrypted password could be stored, for example, in the *shadow* file. There are other systems for protecting passwords of users, such as the *Trusted System* of HP but for now, we just know that the password is not in sight for anybody.

Deleting a user

We will do it with the command *userdel*.

Example:

>[root@noname00 /]# userdel -r user1

The above order has eliminated the system account, including its working directory.

Deleting a group

With *groupdel Name_of_the_group* we will delete a group.

Modify a user's password

If we are the *root* user, with the command *passwd Name_of_the_user* will change the password of an user. If we change our own password, execute the *passwd* command without any parameters.

Example:

>[user1@noname00 ~]$ passwd
>Changing the password of the user user1.
>Changing the password for user1.
>(current) password of UNIX:
>New UNIX password:
>Retype the new UNIX password:
>passwd: all authentication tokens updated successfully.
>[user1@noname00 ~]$

Managing groups

With the command *gpasswd* we can appoint a manager is to be responsible for adding users to group and organize appropriate permissions. The *root* user is responsible for deciding who is the administrator group.

Example:

```
[root@noname00 ~]#  gpasswd -a oracle dba
Adding user oracle to group dba
[root@noname00 ~]# id oracle
uid=1008(oracle) gid=1010(oinstall) groups=1010(oinstall),1008(dba)
context=root:system_r:unconfined_t:SystemLow-SystemHigh
[root@noname00 ~]#
```

Get the user identifiers and group membership for a user

The command *id* will show us this information.

Example:

```
[root@noname00 /]# id user1
uid=601(user1) gid=601(user1) groups=601(user1)
[root@noname00 /]# id
uid=0(root) gid=0(root)
groups=0(root),1(bin),2(daemon),3(sys),4(adm),6(disk),10(wheel)
[root@noname00 /]#
```

Switch user

If we have more than one account in the system, it is possible that at some point we want to switch users without closing the current session. We will succeed with the command *su*.

Example:

```
[user1@noname00 ~]$ id
uid=601(user1) gid=601(user1) groups=601(user1)
[user1@noname00 ~]$ su David
Password:
[David@noname00 usuer1]$ id
uid=500(David) gid=500(David) groups=6(disk),500(David)
[David@noname00 user1]$
```

In the above example, we have gone from being "user1" to the user "David", however, is not an instruction equivalent to the start of a session, which loads the user's profile (environment variables, execution of logon scripts, aliases, etc.). To get a login as if we star a session we will type *su – Name_of_the_user.*

Example:

>[user1@noname00 ~]$ su - David
>Password:
>Hello David
>[David@noname00 ~]$

If we look at log on with the user *David*, has displayed a message that we have not seen in the example above: *Hello David*. This is because it has run a script programmed into the login profile of this user. The same would apply, for example, assigning a value to some environment variables that a software needs and uses the user *David*, so you can run correctly.

Later will explain how to modify the login script.

Searching for errors in the configuration files of passwords and groups

pwck y *grpck*, will search errors in the files */etc/passwd* y */etc/group*, respectively.

Example:

>[root@noname00 ~]# pwck
>user adm: the directory /var/adm does not exist
>user uucp: the directory /var/spool/uucp does not exist
>user gopher: the directory /var/gopher does not exist
>user ftp: the directory /var/ftp does not exist
>user avahi-autoipd: the directory /var/lib/avahi-autoipd does not exist
>pwck: without changes

[root@noname00 ~]#

[root@noname00 ~]# grpck
'David' is a member of the 'disk' group in /etc/group but not in /etc/gshadow
[root@noname00 ~]#

Use a different shell from the current

Since there are different Shells (Bourne Shell, C Shell, Korn Shell, etc.). It is possible that a user is more accustomed to a shell than another. A shell is an interface between the user and the system that allows to type commands, the system interprets them, and returns its result in the same shell.

Example:

[user1@noname00 ~]$ chsh -s /bin/ksh
Changing shell for user1.
Password:
It has changed the shell.
[user1@noname00 ~]$

Managing permissions on files and directories

As the concepts explained in the previous chapter, a directory or file can have permissions for reading, writing and execution, but are not permanent because it can be modified. Here are some commands related to the permissions on files and directories:

Modify the permissions of reading, writing and execution of a file

chmod change the permissions of reading, writing and execution of a file. Only the file's owner, manager of groups of or the system administrator can perform this action.

Examples:

> We will use the file *file.txt* to modify its permissions. Initially have the following:
>
> > [user1@noname00 myfiles]$ ls -la
> > total 8
> > drwxrwxr-x 2 user1 user1   24 nov 8 06:46 .
> > drwx------ 7 user1 user1 4096 nov 8 06:46 ..
> > **-rw-rw-r--** 1 user1 user1   5 nov 8 06:46 file.txt
> > [user1@noname00 myfiles]$
>
> ➢ Remove the read permission for the owner of the file:
>
> > [user1@noname00 myfiles]$ chmod u-r file.txt
>
> > With this order, permits are of follows:

>   --w-rw-r-- 1 user1 user1   5 nov 8 06:46 file.txt

As we see, has disappeared the first "r".

> Assign the read permission for the owner of the file:

>   [user1@noname00 myfiles]$ chmod u+r file.txt

Now the permissions revert to the original.

In the above examples, "u" indicates that allocate or unallocate permissions for the owner of the file, the same way, "g" would do the same for the group (chmod g+r file.txt) and "o" for the remainder of users (chmod o+r file.txt).

If instead of modify the permissions of reading, we would like to change the writing permissions, instead of "r" would use "w" (chmod g-w file.txt). The "x" has the same function but on the execution.

Example:

> We change to the user "David" and we try to read a file that belongs to the user "user1" without having permits to do so by not belong to the same group or be the owner of the file:

>   [user1@noname00 myfiles]$ ls -la
>   total 8
>   drwxrwxr-x 2 user1 user1   24 nov 8 06:46 .
>   drwx------ 7 user1 user1 4096 nov 8 06:57 ..
>   -rw-rw---- 1 user1 user1   5 nov 8 06:46 file.txt
>   [user1@noname00 myfiles]$

>   [user1@noname00 myfiles]$ su David
>   Password:
>   [David@noname00 myfiles]$ cat file.txt
>   cat: file.txt: Permission denied
>   [David@noname00 myfiles]$

In this case, so that the user David can read the file, the file should have read permissions for other users.

There is also a form of numerical change the permissions on a file under the rules of the following table

Permission	Value
Owners File	
Read	400
Write	200
Execution	100
The group the file	
Read	40
Write	20
Execution	10
Other users	
Read	4
Write	2
Execution	1

That is, we could assign all the permissions to the owner, reading and writing to the group and read only to other users, as seen below:

```
[user1@noname00 myfiles]$ chmod 764 file.txt
[user1@noname00 myfiles]$ ls -la
total 8
drwxrwxr-x 2 user1 user1   24 nov  8 06:46 .
drwx------ 7 user1 user1 4096 nov  8 06:59 ..
-rwxrw-r-- 1 user1 user1    5 nov  8 06:46 file.txt
[user1@noname00 myfiles]$
```

The explanation of the above example is the following:

- All permissions to the owner: 400+200+100 = 700
- Reading and writing to the group: 40+20=60
- Read to other users: 4
- Parameter that we have send to chmod: 700+60+4=**764**

Assign permissions using ACL

Access Control Lists o ACL is responsible for providing a set of permissions to a file according to the user who is using it. This philosophy also applies to the directories. Its operation is as follows:

- We create the file "test.txt" with the following permissions:

    ```
    [root@noname00 tmp]# ls -la |grep -i test
    -rw-r--r-- 1 root    root      7 nov  2 11:07 test.txt
    [root@noname00 tmp]#
    ```

- Assign permissions to read, write and execute for the user "user1"

    ```
    [root@noname00 ACL]# setfacl -m u:user1:rwx /tmp/test.txt
    [root@noname00 ACL]#
    ```

- If we now look at the file permissions, we will see the symbol "+":

    ```
    [root@noname00 ACL]# ls -la /tmp/test.txt
    -rw-rwxr--+ 1 root root 7 nov  2 11:07 /tmp/test.txt
    [root@noname00 ACL]#
    ```

- We review the ACL permissions assigned to the file:

    ```
    [root@noname00 ACL]# getfacl /tmp/test.txt
    getfacl: Removing leading '/' from absolute path names
    # file: tmp/test.txt
    # owner: root
    # group: root
    user::rw-
    user:user1:rwx
    group::r--
    ```

mask::rwx
other::r--

- And finally, we eliminate it:

    [root@noname00 ACL]# setfacl -x u:user1 /tmp/test.txt

    [root@noname00 ACL]# getfacl /tmp/test.txt
    getfacl: Removing leading '/' from absolute path names
    # file: tmp/test.txt
    # owner: root
    # group: root
    user::rw-
    group::r--
    mask::r--
    other::r--

    [root@noname00 ACL]#

Permission *setuid*

With such permission we can execute commands as if we were the *root* user, temporarily. For example, a user does not have to be able to change the password of another user, but it has to be able to modify his own, however, the password file is common to all users (/etc/passwd), further, the owner and the group of this file corresponds to the *root* user and this can only have write permissions.

    [root@noname00]# ls -la /etc/passwd
    -rw-r--r-- 1 **root root** 2120 nov 8 06:46 /etc/passwd
    [root@noname00]#

So, how can a user change their password and reflect changes in the passwd file? By permission *setuid*, simulating that is the *root* user who is running the command *passwd*.

This permission is represented by the letter "s":

    [root@noname00]# ls -la /usr/bin/passwd
    -rw**s**r-xr-x 1 root root 29368 abr 8 2008 /usr/bin/passwd

[root@noname00]#

If we want to assign this in a numerical manner, we use the value 4000 (chmod 4764 file.txt).

[user1@noname00 myfiles]$ chmod 4764 file.txt
[user1@noname00 myfiles]$ ls -al
total 8
drwxrwxr-x 2 user1 user1   24 nov 8 06:46 .
drwx------ 7 user1 user1 4096 nov 8 06:59 ..
-rwsrw-r-- 1 user1 user1   5 nov 8 06:46 file.txt
[user1@noname00 myfiles]$

Permission *setgid*

This permit is the equivalent of *setuid*, but applied to groups. The letter "s" appears in the groups permission section.

If we want to assign this in a numerical manner, we use the value 2000 (chmod 2764 file.txt).

[user1@noname00 myfiles]$ ls -al
total 8
drwxrwxr-x 2 user1 user1   24 nov 8 06:46 .
drwx------ 7 user1 user1 4096 nov 8 06:59 ..
-rwxrwSr-- 1 user1 user1   5 nov 8 06:46 file.txt
[user1@noname00 myfiles]$

Permission *sticky-bit*

Initially, the permissions for this flag is used to load a program into memory and leave it running, regardless of whether a user has finished using it, and that was achieved was not having to load each time you need to run. However, technological developments have made this permission has other uses in files and directories. If we assign the permissions to a directory that contains the files may be deleted or renamed by:

- The owner of the file.
- The owner of the file directory.
- The *root* user.

This permission is often used in directories that are used by more than one user, such as /tmp or /var/tmp, for example, and is represented by the letter "t".

    [root@noname00 myfiles]# ls -ld /tmp
    drwxrwxrw**t** 73 root root 8192 nov 8 07:17 /tmp
    [root@noname00 myfiles]#

If we want to assign permission *sticky-bit* in numerical form, we will use the number 1000:

    [user1@noname00 myfiles]$ ls -la
    total 8
    drwxrwxr-x 2 user1 user1   24 nov 8 06:46 .
    drwx------ 7 user1 user1 4096 nov 8 06:59 ..
    -rwxrw-r-T 1 user1 user1   5 nov 8 06:46 file.txt
    [user1@noname00 myfiles]$

    [user1@noname00 ~]$ chmod 1775 myfiles/
    [user1@noname00 ~]$ ls -la |grep fil
    drwxrwxr-t 2 user1 user1   24 nov 8 08:10 file.txt
    [user1@noname00 ~]$

Changing the group and owner of a file

chgrp is used to replace the current group that belongs a file by a new group. The syntax is as follows:

    chgrp group file
    chgrp -R group directory

However, there is another more powerful command: *chown*. It is used as follows:

chown user:group file

Example:

```
[root@noname00 myfiles]# ls -la
total 8
drwxrwxr-x 2 user1 user1   24 nov  8 06:46 .
drwx------ 7 user1 user1 4096 nov  8 06:59 ..
-rwxrw-r-- 1 user1 user1    5 nov  8 06:46 file.txt
[root@noname00 myfiles]# chown David:David file.txt
[root@noname00 myfiles]# ls -la
total 8
drwxrwxr-x 2 user1 user1   24 nov  8 06:46 .
drwx------ 7 user1 user1 4096 nov  8 06:59 ..
-rwxrw-r-- 1 David   David    5 nov  8 06:46 file.txt
[root@noname00 myfiles]#
```

Now, we do it recursively, that is, we change the owner's home directory and all it has below:

```
[root@noname00 myfiles]# cd ..
[root@noname00 user1]# chown -R user1:user1 myfiles
```

sudo configuration

This command is used to execute commands with privileges of another user. To do so, the system administrator must configure the file *sudoers*, which is usually located in the directory */etc*.

Example:

> We try to stop one of the network interfaces with the user "user1."

```
[user1@noname00 ~]$ id
uid=601(user1) gid=601(user1) groups=601(user1)
[user1@noname00 ~]$ /sbin/ifconfig eth1 down
SIOCSIFFLAGS: Permission denied
```

> [user1@noname00 ~]$
- As we can see, this user does not have permission to do so, since only *root* can manage the network. However, we will use *sudo* from the user *user1* to stop this interface:

> [user1@noname00 ~]$ sudo -u root /sbin/ifconfig eth1 down
> [sudo] password for user1:
> **user1 is not in the sudoers file.** This incident will be reported.
> [user1@noname00 ~]$

Now we have encountered some security mechanisms that have prevented us to perform this action. The *root* user must configure the file */etc/sudoers* with the commands that can execute the differents users of the system. It is not necessary to say, for the safety of the system is important to protect this file:

> [user1@noname00 ~]$ ls -la /etc/sudoers
> -r--r----- 1 root root 3344 jun 1 09:40 /etc/sudoers
> [user1@noname00 ~]$

Then we will edit the file *sudoers* for the user *user1* can stop or start a network interface. In the following output of the command *cat* have been removed all entries that do not interest us in order to facilitate the explanation:

> [root@noname00 ~]# cat /etc/sudoers
> # We create an alias for a set of users. Users must be separated by commas.
> User_Alias USERS = user1
>
> # We create another alias for a set of commands.
> Cmnd_Alias ADMNET = /sbin/ifconfig
>
> # We define privileges. In this case, all users located in the alias "USERS", can run without requesting a password, all commands defined by the alias "ADMNET"
> USERS ALL= NOPASSWD:ADMNET
> [user1@noname00 ~]$

Once configured, we turn to run a test:

```
[user1@noname00 ~]$ sudo -u root /sbin/ifconfig eth1 down
[user1@noname00 ~]$ /sbin/ifconfig
lo        Link encap:Local Loopback
          inet addr:127.0.0.1  Mask:255.0.0.0
          inet6 addr: ::1/128 Scope:Host
          UP LOOPBACK RUNNING  MTU:16436  Metric:1
          RX packets:2816 errors:0 dropped:0 overruns:0 frame:0
          TX packets:2816 errors:0 dropped:0 overruns:0 carrier:0
          collisions:0 txqueuelen:0
          RX bytes:210976 (206.0 KiB)  TX bytes:210976 (206.0 KiB)

vmnet0    Link encap:Ethernet  HWaddr 00:18:F3:64:59:CD
          inet addr:192.168.1.3  Bcast:192.168.1.255  Mask:255.255.255.0
          inet6 addr: fe80::218:f3ff:fe64:59cd/64 Scope:Link
          UP BROADCAST RUNNING MULTICAST  MTU:1500  Metric:1
          RX packets:2484 errors:0 dropped:0 overruns:0 frame:0
          TX packets:2716 errors:0 dropped:0 overruns:0 carrier:0
          collisions:0 txqueuelen:0
          RX bytes:1842129 (1.7 MiB)  TX bytes:486568 (475.1 KiB)

vmnet1    Link encap:Ethernet  HWaddr 00:50:56:C0:00:01
          inet addr:172.16.165.1  Bcast:172.16.165.255  Mask:255.255.255.0
          inet6 addr: fe80::250:56ff:fec0:1/64 Scope:Link
          UP BROADCAST RUNNING MULTICAST  MTU:1500  Metric:1
          RX packets:0 errors:0 dropped:0 overruns:0 frame:0
          TX packets:27 errors:0 dropped:0 overruns:0 carrier:0
          collisions:0 txqueuelen:1000
          RX bytes:0 (0.0 b)  TX bytes:0 (0.0 b)

vmnet8    Link encap:Ethernet  HWaddr 00:50:56:C0:00:08
          inet addr:172.16.166.1  Bcast:172.16.166.255  Mask:255.255.255.0
          inet6 addr: fe80::250:56ff:fec0:8/64 Scope:Link
          UP BROADCAST RUNNING MULTICAST  MTU:1500  Metric:1
          RX packets:0 errors:0 dropped:0 overruns:0 frame:0
          TX packets:27 errors:0 dropped:0 overruns:0 carrier:0
          collisions:0 txqueuelen:1000
          RX bytes:0 (0.0 b)  TX bytes:0 (0.0 b)

[user1@noname00 ~]$
```

As we see, the command has not asked us a password, or have given us permission error and no longer appears the network interface *eth1*. Then, we start the interface with the same user:

```
[user1@noname00 ~]$ sudo -u root /sbin/ifconfig eth1 up
[user1@noname00 ~]$ /sbin/ifconfig
eth1      Link encap:Ethernet  HWaddr 00:18:F3:64:59:CD
          inet addr:192.168.1.2  Bcast:192.168.1.255  Mask:255.255.255.0
          inet6 addr: fe80::218:f3ff:fe64:59cd/64 Scope:Link
          UP BROADCAST RUNNING PROMISC MULTICAST  MTU:1500  Metric:1
          RX packets:2504 errors:0 dropped:0 overruns:0 frame:0
          TX packets:2721 errors:0 dropped:0 overruns:0 carrier:0
          collisions:0 txqueuelen:1000
          RX bytes:1844830 (1.7 MiB)  TX bytes:493313 (481.7 KiB)
          Interrupt:16

lo        Link encap:Local Loopback
          inet addr:127.0.0.1  Mask:255.0.0.0
          inet6 addr: ::1/128 Scope:Host
          UP LOOPBACK RUNNING  MTU:16436  Metric:1
          RX packets:2816 errors:0 dropped:0 overruns:0 frame:0
          TX packets:2816 errors:0 dropped:0 overruns:0 carrier:0
          collisions:0 txqueuelen:0
          RX bytes:210976 (206.0 KiB)  TX bytes:210976 (206.0 KiB)

vmnet0    Link encap:Ethernet  HWaddr 00:18:F3:64:59:CD
          inet addr:192.168.1.3  Bcast:192.168.1.255  Mask:255.255.255.0
          inet6 addr: fe80::218:f3ff:fe64:59cd/64 Scope:Link
          UP BROADCAST RUNNING MULTICAST  MTU:1500  Metric:1
          RX packets:2484 errors:0 dropped:0 overruns:0 frame:0
          TX packets:2716 errors:0 dropped:0 overruns:0 carrier:0
          collisions:0 txqueuelen:0
          RX bytes:1842129 (1.7 MiB)  TX bytes:486568 (475.1 KiB)

vmnet1    Link encap:Ethernet  HWaddr 00:50:56:C0:00:01
          inet addr:172.16.165.1  Bcast:172.16.165.255  Mask:255.255.255.0
          inet6 addr: fe80::250:56ff:fec0:1/64 Scope:Link
```

```
          UP BROADCAST RUNNING MULTICAST  MTU:1500  Metric:1
          RX packets:0 errors:0 dropped:0 overruns:0 frame:0
          TX packets:27 errors:0 dropped:0 overruns:0 carrier:0
          collisions:0 txqueuelen:1000
          RX bytes:0 (0.0 b)  TX bytes:0 (0.0 b)

vmnet8    Link encap:Ethernet  HWaddr 00:50:56:C0:00:08
          inet addr:172.16.166.1  Bcast:172.16.166.255  Mask:255.255.255.0
          inet6 addr: fe80::250:56ff:fec0:8/64 Scope:Link
          UP BROADCAST RUNNING MULTICAST  MTU:1500  Metric:1
          RX packets:0 errors:0 dropped:0 overruns:0 frame:0
          TX packets:27 errors:0 dropped:0 overruns:0 carrier:0
          collisions:0 txqueuelen:1000
          RX bytes:0 (0.0 b)  TX bytes:0 (0.0 b)

[user1@noname00 ~]$
```

We could use this command, for example, to create a user can perform some maintenance tasks. Imagine a service that must be working for most of the day, as a website in which is sold tickets for movies, theatre, concerts, etc. and that, therefore, the time window that has the least impact on the service occurs during late night, that is when we can schedule some maintenance tasks, such as reboot the server. However, system administrators are not working for around the clock, but in our company we have a department of operators who have no knowledge of administration or a privileged user, but could run a few scripts that administrators have prepared them to perform these functions. In this way we achieve a stable system and without running the risk of an inexperienced person to execute a command that does not want for fear of misuse of it.

File system administration

Concepts

So far, we have seen as copy, move, delete, create links to files and other functions through various commands on the system but, after these commands, there is a file structure that can store the information.

An inode is a structure that stores information about a file, but not the actual file. The information that store is:

- Identifier of the device that contains the file system.
- Inode number: Each has its unique identifier within the table of inodes.
- File type.
- Owner and group of the file.
- Permissions (rwx).
- Creation date.
- Size of the file.
- Number of links associated with the same inode.

The inodes table is created during the system boot and is used for commands like *find* in order to expedite the search of information about files.

The number of inodes depends on the size of each inode. With *"df -i"* we can know the number of inodes we have in a file system:

```
[usuario1@noname00 ~]$ df -i
S.ficheros            Nodos-i NUsados  NLibres NUso% Montado en
/dev/sda2              224000   10496   213504    5% /
/dev/mapper/vg00-lvvar
                     12288000   12484 12275516    1% /var
/dev/mapper/vg00-lvtmp
                     10223616     726 10222890    1% /tmp
/dev/mapper/vg00-lvusr
                     20480000  209292 20270708    2% /usr
/dev/mapper/vg00-lvopt
                    191070208   82968 190987240   1% /opt
/dev/mapper/vg00-lvhome
                     12288000   20148 12267852    1% /home
tmpfs                  502443       6   502437    1% /dev/shm
```

If we exhaust the number of inodes because we keep a large number of files in the filesystem or have created it with a low number of inodes, we get an error message of not enough space in the filesystem, even if we still see remaining free space on the filesystem (but no free inodes).

Each operating system and filesystem type has its own procedure to set the inode number of a filesystem. For example, on RedHat and ext4 filesystem type, would be as follows:

    mkfs.ext4 **-N 250000** -j -T largefile /dev/vg00/lvol1

With the -N 250000 parameter we are setting the number of inodes when we are creating the filesystem.

Creating a partition, a file system, mount the file system and use it

In the UNIX world there is wide variety of files systems: ext3, ext4, XFS, ReiserFS, xfs, vxfs, etc. each with its unique properties and commands. There are also different software to manage the partitions where the file system will be mount. Some of the most widely used are *fdisk* and *parted*.

Example of creating a file system:

- First step: We create the disk partition on which the file will be created.

   [root@noname00 /]# fdisk /dev/sdb
   Device contains neither a valid DOS partition table, nor Sun, SGI or OSF disklabel
   Building a new DOS disklabel. Changes will remain in memory only,
   until you decide to write them. After that, of course, the previous
   content won't be recoverable.

   The number of cylinders for this disk is set to 2088.
   There is nothing wrong with that, but this is larger than 1024,
   and could in certain setups cause problems with:
   1) software that runs at boot time (e.g., old versions of LILO)
   2) booting and partitioning software from other OSs

(e.g., DOS FDISK, OS/2 FDISK)
Warning: invalid flag 0x0000 of partition table 4 will be corrected by w(rite)

Command (m for help): m
Command action
   a   toggle a bootable flag
   b   edit bsd disklabel
   c   toggle the dos compatibility flag
   d   delete a partition
   l   list known partition types
   m   print this menu
   n   add a new partition
   o   create a new empty DOS partition table
   p   print the partition table
   q   quit without saving changes
   s   create a new empty Sun disklabel
   t   change a partition's system id
   u   change display/entry units
   v   verify the partition table
   w   write table to disk and exit
   x   extra functionality (experts only)

Command (m for help): n
Command action
   e   extended
   p   primary partition (1-4)
p
Partition number (1-4): 1
First cylinder (1-2088, default 1):
Using default value 1
Last cylinder or +size or +sizeM or +sizeK (1-2088, default 2088):
Using default value 2088

Command (m for help): p

Disk /dev/sdb: 17.1 GB, 17179869184 bytes
255 heads, 63 sectors/track, 2088 cylinders
Units = cylinders of 16065 * 512 = 8225280 bytes

   Device Boot   Start   End   Blocks   Id System

```
/dev/sdb1            1      2088   16771828+  83  Linux

Command (m for help): t
Selected partition 1
Hex code (type L to list codes): l

 0  Empty          1e  Hidden W95 FAT1 80  Old Minix      be  Solaris boot
 1  FAT12          24  NEC DOS         81  Minix / old Lin bf  Solaris
 2  XENIX root     39  Plan 9          82  Linux swap / So c1  DRDOS/sec (FAT-
 3  XENIX usr      3c  PartitionMagic  83  Linux           c4  DRDOS/sec (FAT-
 4  FAT16 <32M     40  Venix 80286     84  OS/2 hidden C:  c6  DRDOS/sec (FAT-
 5  Extended       41  PPC PReP Boot   85  Linux extended  c7  Syrinx
 6  FAT16          42  SFS             86  NTFS volume set da  Non-FS data
 7  HPFS/NTFS      4d  QNX4.x          87  NTFS volume set db  CP/M / CTOS /
 8  AIX            4e  QNX4.x 2nd part 88  Linux plaintext de  Dell Utility
 9  AIX bootable   4f  QNX4.x 3rd part 8e  Linux LVM       df  BootIt
 a  OS/2 Boot Manag 50  OnTrack DM     93  Amoeba          e1  DOS access
 b  W95 FAT32      51  OnTrack DM6 Aux 94  Amoeba BBT      e3  DOS R/O
 c  W95 FAT32 (LBA) 52  CP/M           9f  BSD/OS          e4  SpeedStor
 e  W95 FAT16 (LBA) 53  OnTrack DM6 Aux a0  IBM Thinkpad hi eb  BeOS fs
 f  W95 Ext'd (LBA) 54  OnTrackDM6     a5  FreeBSD         ee  EFI GPT
10  OPUS           55  EZ-Drive        a6  OpenBSD         ef  EFI (FAT-12/16/
11  Hidden FAT12   56  Golden Bow      a7  NeXTSTEP        f0  Linux/PA-RISC b
12  Compaq diagnost 5c  Priam Edisk    a8  Darwin UFS      f1  SpeedStor
14  Hidden FAT16 <3 61  SpeedStor      a9  NetBSD          f4  SpeedStor
16  Hidden FAT16   63  GNU HURD or Sys ab  Darwin boot     f2  DOS secondary
17  Hidden HPFS/NTF 64  Novell Netware b7  BSDI fs         fd  Linux raid auto
18  AST SmartSleep 65  Novell Netware  b8  BSDI swap       fe  LANstep
1b  Hidden W95 FAT3 70  DiskSecure Mult bb  Boot Wizard hid ff  BBT
1c  Hidden W95 FAT3 75  PC/IX
Hex code (type L to list codes): 8e
Changed system type of partition 1 to 8e (Linux LVM)

Command (m for help): p
```

```
Disk /dev/sdb: 17.1 GB, 17179869184 bytes
255 heads, 63 sectors/track, 2088 cylinders
Units = cylinders of 16065 * 512 = 8225280 bytes

   Device Boot    Start      End    Blocks  Id  System
/dev/sdb1           1       2088  16771828+  8e  Linux LVM

Command (m for help): w
The partition table has been altered!

Calling ioctl() to re-read partition table.
Syncing disks.
[root@noname00 /]# exit

Script done on mié 20 ago 2008 14:43:44 CEST
[root@noname00 /]#
```

In the example we have just seen has created a *LVM* partition.

The *fdisk -l* command displays a list of all the partitions on the system.

> **Second step:** After creating the partition, we create the file system. As mentioned above, there are many types of file system with its own unique commands. We will create a FS type ext3 with the *journaling* option, to achieve better performance and because it can be expanded without being unmounted. All this under Linux RedHat system:

```
mkfs.ext3 -j -T largefile /dev/vg01/lvol1
```

Another example of creating a file system type *vxfs* (Veritas file system) in an HP-UX:

```
newfs -F vxfs -b 8192 /dev/vgas02/rlvol12
version 5 layout
2097152 sectors, 262144 blocks of size 8192, log size 2048 blocks
unlimited inodes, largefiles not supported
262144 data blocks, 260056 free data blocks
8 allocation units of 32768 blocks, 32768 data blocks
```

We could go on writing examples with each of the different types of file systems, but the objective of this book is to have clear the concepts, the steps to be followed and not explaining the operation of each of the different existing technologies related with file systems. Each of them has been supplemented with their corresponding procedures manual and is the system administrator who has to choose its means of training for the use of so many diverse and constantly evolving technologies.

> Once we have created the file system, we will mount it so that we can use it. To do this, we have the command *mount*.

>> mount [options] -t type_of_filesystem mount_point

Example:

>> [root@noname00 ~]# mount -t ext3 /dev/sda5 /Aplication1
>> [root@noname00 ~]#

>> With this action we just to mount an ext3 filesystem type, whose device is /dev/sda1 in the directory /Aplicación1. Now we can perform any action on the files that are below this directory (copy, move, delete, assign permissions, etc.).

If we have forgotten to include some feature during the creation of the filesystem, we can modify its properties. To cite two examples, in linux sistems exists the order *tune2fs*, while in HP-UX we have *fsadm*. Example:

>> [root@noname00 /]# tune2fs -l /dev/mapper/vgGEAas-lvol2
>> tune2fs 1.39 (29-May-2006)
>> Filesystem volume name: <none>
>> Last mounted on: <not available>
>> Filesystem UUID: c2ca12db-8172-4a76-a9ed-c5ffd68b27b2
>> Filesystem magic number: 0xEF53
>> Filesystem revision #:   1 (dynamic)
>> Filesystem features: has_journal resize_inode dir_index filetype needs_recovery sparse_super large_file
>> Default mount options: (none)

```
Filesystem state:        clean
Errors behavior:         Continue
Filesystem OS type:      Linux
Inode count:             1441792
Block count:             2883584
Reserved block count:    144172
Free blocks:             714916
Free inodes:             1287429
First block:             0
Block size:              4096
Fragment size:           4096
Reserved GDT blocks:     575
Blocks per group:        32768
Fragments per group:     32768
Inodes per group:        16384
Inode blocks per group:  512
Filesystem created:      Thu Mar 19 09:07:29 2009
Last mount time:         Thu Jul 30 12:22:05 2009
Last write time:         Thu Jul 30 12:22:05 2009
Mount count:             8
Maximum mount count:     36
Last checked:            Thu Mar 19 09:07:29 2009
Check interval:          15552000 (6 months)
Next check after:        Tue Sep 15 10:07:29 2009
Reserved blocks uid:     0 (user root)
Reserved blocks gid:     0 (group root)
First inode:             11
Inode size:              128
Journal inode:           8
First orphan inode:      136705
Default directory hash:  tea
Directory Hash Seed:     26b28e17-dffe-4fd2-85ed-35b39c5db7a0
Journal backup:          inode blocks
[root@noname00 /]#
```

If we want the file systems are mounted during system boot, we must include their entries in the file */etc/fstab*.

Example:

```
[user1@noname00 ~]$ cat /etc/fstab
UUID=c7037588-e094-4452-aeda-91142dbc3229 /           ext3    defaults    1 1
/dev/vg00/lvvar         /var            xfs     defaults    1 2
/dev/vg00/lvtmp         /tmp            xfs     defaults    1 2
/dev/vg00/lvusr         /usr            xfs     defaults    1 2
/dev/vg00/lvopt         /opt            xfs     defaults    1 2
/dev/vg00/lvhome        /home           xfs     defaults    1 2
tmpfs                   /dev/shm        tmpfs   defaults    0 0
devpts                  /dev/pts        devpts  gid=5,mode=620  0 0
sysfs                   /sys            sysfs   defaults    0 0
proc                    /proc           proc    defaults    0 0
/dev/vg00/lvswap        swap            swap    defaults    0 0
```

This file is structured as follows:

- Device
- Mount point.
- Filesystem type
- Mount options:
    - **auto.** It is mounted automatically or with the command *mount -a*.
    - **noauto.** It is not mounted automatically (as a removable device).
    - **defaults.** This value represents a set of mounting options: async, auto, dev, exec, nouser, rw y suid.
    - **dev.** It refers to a local device.
    - **exec.** Allowing execution of binaries and scripts.
    - **nouser.** The file system can only be mounted by root.
    - **owner.** The user who mount the FS is also its owner.
    - **ro.** Read only.
    - **rw.** Read and write.
    - **suid.** *suid* bits can be used.
    - **sync.** Writing synchronous.
- The value of the next field can be 0 or 1. If it is 1, the system copies "Dump" will copy the information iofn this file system.
- The last field checks the consistency of the file system. If 0, it will not be checked during boot.

Depending on the type of filesystem that we are using, we will find different commands for resizing (resize2fs, fsadm, xfsgrowfs, are just some examples) or repairing (fsck o xfs_repair, for example).

Create the entry of a new device in the system

mknod is the command that is responsible for performing this function. It is useful when we have visibility of a new LUN or adding a new disk. *mknod* values must be unique.

>Command syntax:
>
>>mknod /dev/my_device type major minor
>>
>>major and minor refers to the maximum and minimum number of devices of the same type that may exist.
>
>Example:
>
>>mknod /dev/vgdatabase/group c 64 0x*hh*0000
>
>*hh* is the only value which commented earlier.

Network Filesystem Service (NFS)

NFS is a system that allows to use, locally, filesystems shared by a remote server. The operation of the system is based on a client-server application, that is, the server is responsible to share a filesystem and clients communicate with the application server to access the data shared file system.

The implementation of NFS can vary from one UNIX system to another, that is, is not the same NFS configuration on a Solaris operating system that in an HP-UX but, as a concept, we will indicate how to set it in a Solaris, in honor of the creator of this system: SUN Microsystems.

- **NFS on the server:** First, we must ensure that the *nfsd* daemon is started, whether it is not, we can start as follows:

    /etc/init.d/nfs.server start

  Then we will proceed to share the file system */Aplication1* in read and write mode, for servers "Server1" and "Server2", executing the following instruction:

    [root@noname00 ~]# share -f NFS -o rw=Server1,Server2 /Aplication1

  Obviously, in the system that contains the NFS server, the filesystem */Aplication1* must be mounted in advance.

  The options that can be put behind the parameter "-o" are as follows:

  > anon: Relates, anonymously, requests from users.
  > nosuid: Prevents applications to run as *setuid*.
  > ro: Read only.
  > root: We have *root* privileges on the remote FS.
  > rw: Reading and writing.

  The directories that are shared, are identified in */etc/dfs/dfstab*, although the command *dfmounts* of Solaris allows viewing the shared filesystems.

- **NFS on the client:** Like on the server, the client has a daemon that must to be running in order to access the remote file system. This is: */etc/init.d/nfs.client*, */usr/lib/nfs/statd* (statistics) and */usr/lib/nfs/lockd* (daemon blocking NFS). Once started the client, will be mounted filesystems listed in the file */etc/vfstab* of the client machine (if the server's configuration allows it).

  Example:

    Server1:/Aplication1 /Local_Aplication1 nfs yes rw

  If we access to the directory */Local_Aplication1* of the client machine, we will be watching the data contained in the directory */Aplication1* of the remote server.

We can also mount manually the remote filesystem:

   mount -F nfs -o ro Server1:/Aplication1 /Local_Aplication1

where the parameter "-o" you can purchase the following values:

- ro: Read only.
- rw: Reading and writing.
- Hard: The client repeatedly seek to establish the connection if it loses. There is no waiting time.
- Soft: Allowing the interruption of service for timeout. The client will try the connection and will return an error if it fails.
- Bg: Tries to mount a remote FS in the background if the connection fails.

Finally, in terms of NFS is concerned, emphasize that all the commands used belong to the Solaris operating system and the rest of UNIX systems have their equivalent commands to do the same.

Disks in mirror

Concepts

When it is said that a disk is in the mirror, means that there is another disk just like the first one where are constantly replicating all the changes of the original disk. Then, we will get data redundancy and, therefore, always be able to access them although will ruin some of the disks.
Normally, in the super servers, the mirror of the internal disks is performed by hardware, but also can be done by software.

Once mounted the mirror structure, from the system we will see only one logical unit of data access, as if we had only one disk.

The next drawing can serve to enlighten us a little more these concepts:

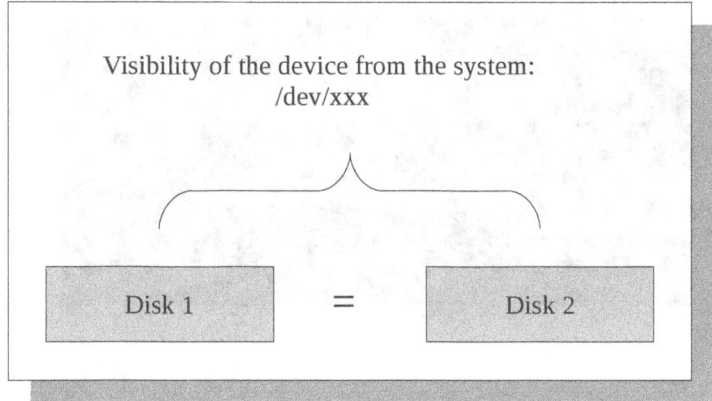

Creating a mirror structure by software

Then we explain how to make a mirror by software on a RedHat system:

The disk /dev/sdb1 will be the mirror of /dev/sda1.

- We boot from from the RedHat DVD to make sure the device is not busy.
- We run the command:

    mdadm --create /dev/md0 --level 1 --raid-devices 2 /dev/sda1 /dev/sdb1

    This creates the metadevice, that is, the device that accesses both discs (original and mirror).

If we would like to add more than one disk, we will execute:

   mdadm --manage /dev/md0 --add /dev/sda3

To check the configuration of all the mirrors, we can display the contents of the file */proc/mdstat* of RedHat:

```
[root@localhost ~]# cat /proc/mdstat
Personalities : [raid1]
md1 : active raid1 hdb2[1] hda2[0]
      3582400 blocks [2/2] [UU]

md0 : active raid1 hdb1[1] hda1[0]
      104320 blocks [2/2] [UU]

unused devices: <none>
[root@localhost ~]#
```

The structure of disks in the mirror is also known as RAID1, although there are other types of RAID, from RAID0 until RAID6 but only RAID1, 5 and 6 are the most widely used at present.
RAID is the acronym Redundant Array of Independent Disks.

Apart from the different RAID configurations, we can complement it with *stripping*. *Stripping* means we will store data evently distributed among all disks, that is to say, if we have two discs, we will save half of a file on a disk and the other half in the other, resulting in a significant performance improvement.

RAID5

This system consists of a set of disks divided into blocks of data, distributing the parity information among the different disks, members of package in order to achieve data redundancy.
When there is a problem in one of the disks, as an error of CRC (**C**yclic **R**edundancy **C**heck), it is possible reconstruct the data using a mathematical calculation from the parity information from the other blocks. If lose more than one block would be lost all data.

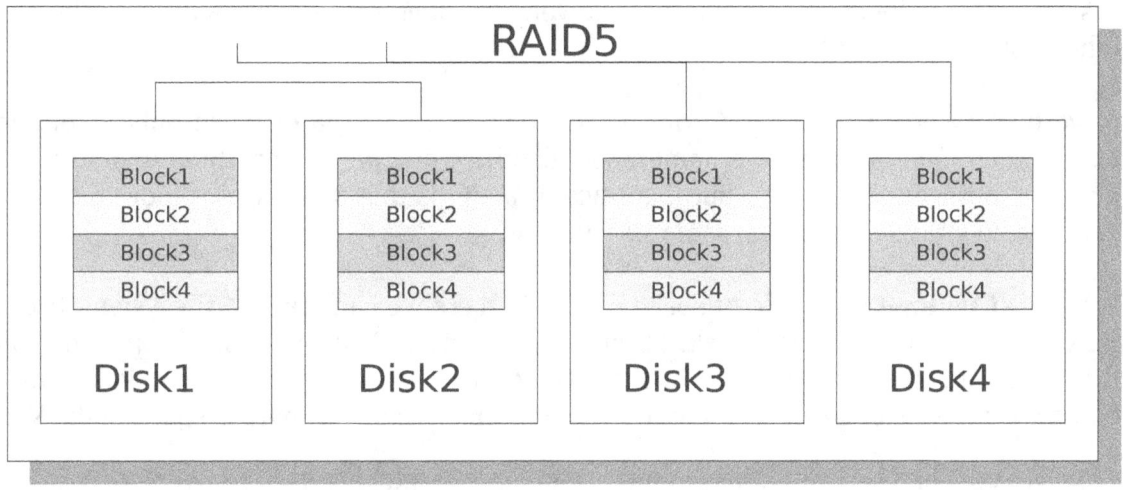

When is serving a request for reading on the Block1 of Disk1, can not meet a similar request on the Bloque2 on the same disk, as it would have to wait, but it may serve a petition on the Block2 of Disk2 because of is used different disk. This is translated into a lower response time in gaining access to information.

Of course, there are technologies of hardware and software of RAID5, but the most common is to use the hardware.

Logical Volume Manager (LVM)

Concepts

Logical Volume Manager is a manager of disk space consists of the following layers:

- Physical disks (PV – physical volume).
- Volume groups (VG).
- Logical Volumes (LV).

A **physical disk** can be an entire disk or a LUN. A LUN is a disk space visible from our system, but it belongs to external disks tower. Our operating system will treat like any other disk.

A **Volume Group** is a grouping of physical disks. In LVM, a disc can only belong to one VG. The VG is assigned a name to be identified and we can create as many as free disks we have in our system, but the grace of a VG is that the space of more than one disk can be grouped under the same structure.

A **Logical Volume** is a piece of space of a VG where we can create a filesystem. It can make use part of a physical disk, an entire disk, more than one disk... depending on their size and distribution space in the VG. We can say that it is the equivalent of a partition and we can create as many LVs as we want, wherever there is space in the VG.

The space of the VG is divided into blocks known as Physical Extents (PE), that is, the space of a Logical Volume must be a multiple of the size of a PE.

In the next image we can see represented graphically what we just explain:

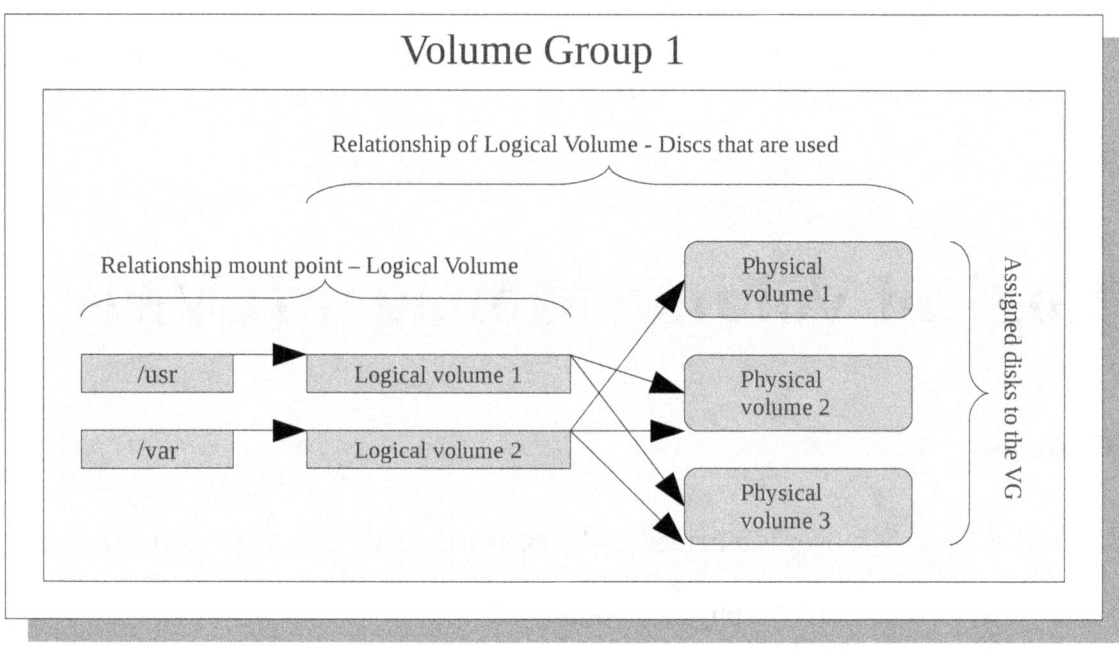

and then, here is a LVM structure already mounted on a system with its different sections marked in bold:

```
[root@noname00 ~]# vgdisplay -v vg00
    Using volume group(s) on command line
    Finding volume group "vg00"
  --- Volume group ---
  VG Name               vg00
  System ID
  Format                lvm2
  Metadata Areas        3
  Metadata Sequence No  7
  VG Access             read/write
  VG Status             resizable
  MAX LV                0
  Cur LV                6
  Open LV               6
  Max PV                0
  Cur PV                3
  Act PV                3
  VG Size               239,41 GB
  PE Size               32,00 MB
  Total PE              7661
  Alloc PE / Size       7658 / 239,31 GB
  Free  PE / Size       3 / 96,00 MB
  VG UUID               73DE9r-rwGz-KOmG-qCZQ-3nIZ-7Z7J-Uz3UYX

  --- Logical volume ---
  LV Name                /dev/vg00/lvvar
  VG Name                vg00
  LV UUID                ewFSSv-0zew-qn74-3MN8-tJYD-lvcB-HfgGYh
  LV Write Access        read/write
  LV Status              available
  # open                 1
  LV Size                11,72 GB
  Current LE             375
  Segments               1
  Allocation             inherit
  Read ahead sectors     auto
  - currently set to     256
  Block device           253:0
```

--- **Logical volume** ---
LV Name /dev/vg00/lvtmp
VG Name vg00
LV UUID 7akx3G-YFsa-Ft0J-cQZJ-KVXq-aa1B-bTqNkY
LV Write Access read/write
LV Status available
open 1
LV Size 9,75 GB
Current LE 312
Segments 1
Allocation inherit
Read ahead sectors auto
- currently set to 256
Block device 253:1

--- **Logical volume** ---
LV Name /dev/vg00/lvusr
VG Name vg00
LV UUID qCB1Fe-FV49-QReg-hJ9M-enPe-57Ia-K17RUg
LV Write Access read/write
LV Status available
open 1
LV Size 19,53 GB
Current LE 625
Segments 1
Allocation inherit
Read ahead sectors auto
- currently set to 256
Block device 253:2

--- **Logical volume** ---
LV Name /dev/vg00/lvopt
VG Name vg00
LV UUID dzmlen-Pw9B-Sn9D-Kk4m-tzcx-nMfa-PpO0lr
LV Write Access read/write
LV Status available
open 1
LV Size 182,22 GB
Current LE 5831
Segments 2

```
  Allocation             inherit
  Read ahead sectors     auto
  - currently set to     256
  Block device           253:3

  --- Logical volume ---
  LV Name                /dev/vg00/lvhome
  VG Name                vg00
  LV UUID                jTkoBb-CR8T-ethA-CVWv-NQVH-EP0P-NjDiP1
  LV Write Access        read/write
  LV Status              available
  # open                 1
  LV Size                11,72 GB
  Current LE             375
  Segments               1
  Allocation             inherit
  Read ahead sectors     auto
  - currently set to     256
  Block device           253:4

  --- Logical volume ---
  LV Name                /dev/vg00/lvswap
  VG Name                vg00
  LV UUID                XQS8ah-7b7a-3Kke-bTPz-7XRN-XEfS-Z83RuP
  LV Write Access        read/write
  LV Status              available
  # open                 1
  LV Size                4,38 GB
  Current LE             140
  Segments               1
  Allocation             inherit
  Read ahead sectors     auto
  - currently set to     256
  Block device           253:5

  --- Physical volumes ---
  PV Name                /dev/sda5
  PV UUID                yXKLi8-Iqkw-QC27-zfpf-KBCb-9iT4-2Goo4J
  PV Status              allocatable
  Total PE / Free PE     3 / 3
```

```
PV Name              /dev/sda3
PV UUID              P9S6KS-DIzG-CNAl-Lcdk-83Mz-VhCT-pmGrau
PV Status            allocatable
Total PE / Free PE   3176 / 0

PV Name              /dev/sdb1
PV UUID              NRRxsB-7xAF-wiGZ-Vkqa-XBpv-yZOY-raPOzb
PV Status            allocatable
Total PE / Free PE   4482 / 0

[root@noname00 ~]#
```

As we can see, each mount point coincides with a Logical Volume:

```
[root@noname00 ~]# mount |grep lv
/dev/mapper/vg00-lvvar on /var type xfs (rw)
/dev/mapper/vg00-lvtmp on /tmp type xfs (rw)
/dev/mapper/vg00-lvusr on /usr type xfs (rw)
/dev/mapper/vg00-lvopt on /opt type xfs (rw)
/dev/mapper/vg00-lvhome on /home type xfs (rw)
[root@noname00 ~]#
```

Creating a LVM structure

Then we attach an example of creating a LVM structure, under HP-UX:

- Creation of the physical volumes to assign a header to each device:

    pvcreate /dev/rdsk/c1t2d0
    pvcreate /dev/rdsk/c0t2d0

- Creating the directory of the new volume called *vgdatabase:*

    mkdir /dev/vgdatabase vgdatabase

- Creating the unique identifier of the device:

    mknod /dev/vgdatabase/group c 64 0x*hh*0000

- Creation of the VG vgdatabase, formed by the disks listed on the first point of this procedure:

    vgcreate /dev/vgdatabase /dev/dsk/c1t2d0
    vgextend /dev/vgdatabase /dev/dsk/c0t2d0

  Instead of doing *vgcreate* and *vgextend*, we could have separated with a space each disk in the order *vgcreate*, but we have thought appropriate to apply the command *vgextend* to show how is joined a new disk.

- Creating the logical volume of 120MB within the vgdatabase VG:

    lvcreate -L 120 -m 1 -s g /dev/vgdatabase

- Creation and mounting the filesystem:
    newfs -F vxfs /dev/vgdatabase/rlvol1
    mount /dev/vgdatabase/lvol1 /mnt1

LVM commands

Expand a file system

    extendfs /dev/vg00/rlvol3

Modify the properties of a logical volume

    lvchange -t 60 /dev/vg00/lvol3

Create a logical volume

lvcreate -L 100 /dev/vg00

Deleting a logical volume

lvremove /dev/vg00/lvol6

Show information of the logical volumes

lvdisplay -v /dev/vg00/lvol1

Creating a mirror of a logical volume

lvextend -m 1 /dev/vg00/lvol3

Deleting a mirror

lvreduce -m 0 /dev/vg00/lvol3

Synchronize two LVS in mirror

lvsync /dev/vg00/lvol1

Increasing the size of a logical volume

lvextend -L 120 /dev/vg00/lvol3

Decreasing the size of a logical volume

lvreduce -L 100 /dev/vg00/lvol3

Create a physical volume

pvcreate /dev/rdisk/disk2

Remove a physical volume

pvremove /dev/rdisk/disk2

Modify the properties of a physical volume

pvchange -a n /dev/disk/disk2

Check the consistency of a physical volume

pvck /dev/disk/disk2

Save the settings of LVM

vgcfgbackup vg00

Restore the LVM configuration

vgcfgrestore -n /dev/vg00 /dev/rdisk/disk2

Just add a new disk that has replaced a broken disk twhich had no mirror or RAID.

Create a VG

vgcreate /dev/vg01 /dev/disk/disk2 /dev/disk/disk3

Remove a VG of the system

vgexport /dev/vg01

Removes a group of volumes in the system and its associated disks

    vgremove /dev/vg00 /dev/disk/disk2

Activate or deactivate a VG

    vgchange -a y /dev/vg00
    vgchange -a n /dev/vg00

Show the configuration of a VG

    vgdisplay -v /dev/vg00

Add a disk to a VG

    vgextend /dev/vg00 /dev/disk/disk2

Importing a VG to a system

    # mkdir /dev/vg04
    # mknod /dev/vg04/group c 640x0n0000
    # vgimport -v /dev/vg04

Remove a disk from a VG

    vgreduce /dev/vg00 /dev/disk/disk2

Move a VG from one server to another

A group of volumes should be only active on one server to prevent data corruption, however, may be the fact that the server where it normally is on, has any impact. So that data remain accessible in high-availability services, the VGs are pointing to external disks also accessible from another server. In order to activate a VG on an alternative system, follow the following steps:

- The first time you create the VG on the original server and each time you change its settings, run the following command:

    vgexport -p -s -m /tmp/VG_name.map /dev/VG_name

    The "-p" argument is important for not removing the VG in the system.

- In the alternate server, we create the *mknod* in the same way that exists on the original server.

    mkdir /dev/VG_name
    mknod /dev/VG_name/group c 64 0x*hh*0000

- We copy the file */tmp/VG_name.map* created in the first step of this procedure, to the alternative server and we run:

    vgimport -s -m /tmp/vgdatabase.map /dev/vgdatabase

- To activate the VG on the new server, we first must disable it in the original:

    vgchange -a n /dev/VG_name

- We activate the VG in the alternate server:

    vgchange -a y /dev/VG_name

- We mount filesystems with the command *mount*:

    mount /dev/VG_name/LV_name/mount_point

Network administration

Concepts

A communications network is made up of elements of hardware and software able to establish communication links in order to exchange data via a communications protocol specified.

Some of the most important hardware elements:

- **Wiring**
- **Switches:** The systems connected to a same switch are part of the same network.
- **Routers:** They are responsible for directing a packet of information to the network address that corresponds.
- **Firewalls:** Establish security policies in the network, that is, let or not a particular type of traffic, protocol or connection from certain servers or networks.
- **Balancers:** They are responsible for distributing traffic between different network addresses that are configured.
- **Proxy:** Is responsible for providing a way out of traffic to a different network. The proxy is the only component connected to another network, so the rest of servers must use it for accessing to another computer located in the external network.
- **Network cards:** Is the hardware component that is responsible for establishing network connections with other devices. They can be wired (Ethernet RJ45), fiber optics or wireless (WiFi).

The elements of software that can be found:

- Programs that also have functions of proxy, firewall or balancer of traffic.
- **Communications protocol:** Are all those rules that are used for two programs,

hardware components or a mixture of both, can exchange data decipherable with each other, this is, the origin and destination have to speak the same language to understand what they are saying and sent the correct information. If the origin and destination are not using the same protocol, can not ever communicate. The most widely used communications protocol at present is TCP/IP (**T**ransmission **C**ontrol **P**rotocol/**I**nternet Protocol). TCP packet contains the information and IP the address where the package is sent.
- Other applications, client server, which communicate with each other through a protocol.

Assembly and operation of a network structure

Following are what might be the actual assembly of a network structure:

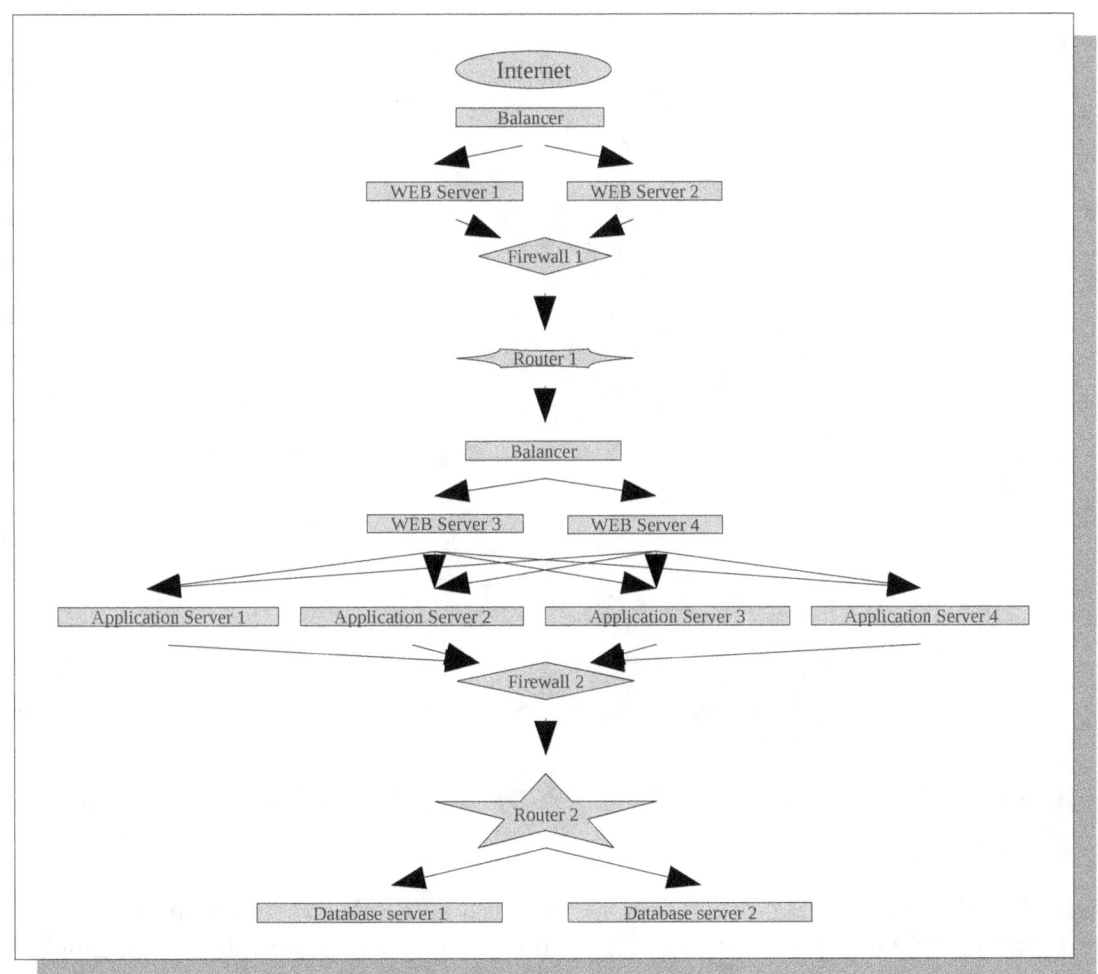

In the previous scheme, a user connects to a website through one of the two web servers to which the balancer redirects the request. Next, we have a firewall that protects the MZ (militarized zone), which contains a balancer to redirect traffic to two other webservers connected to the application servers. In the MZ can not access any Internet user, this means that it is protected from direct external attacks.

The applications collect data that are sent to the database servers, which are also protected by another firewall, and return the result to the website which is consulting the user.

In the example above, and in any communication established, there is: a transmitter, the information sent, the channel through which sends and receiver. In the TCP/IP protocol that structure could be built as follows:

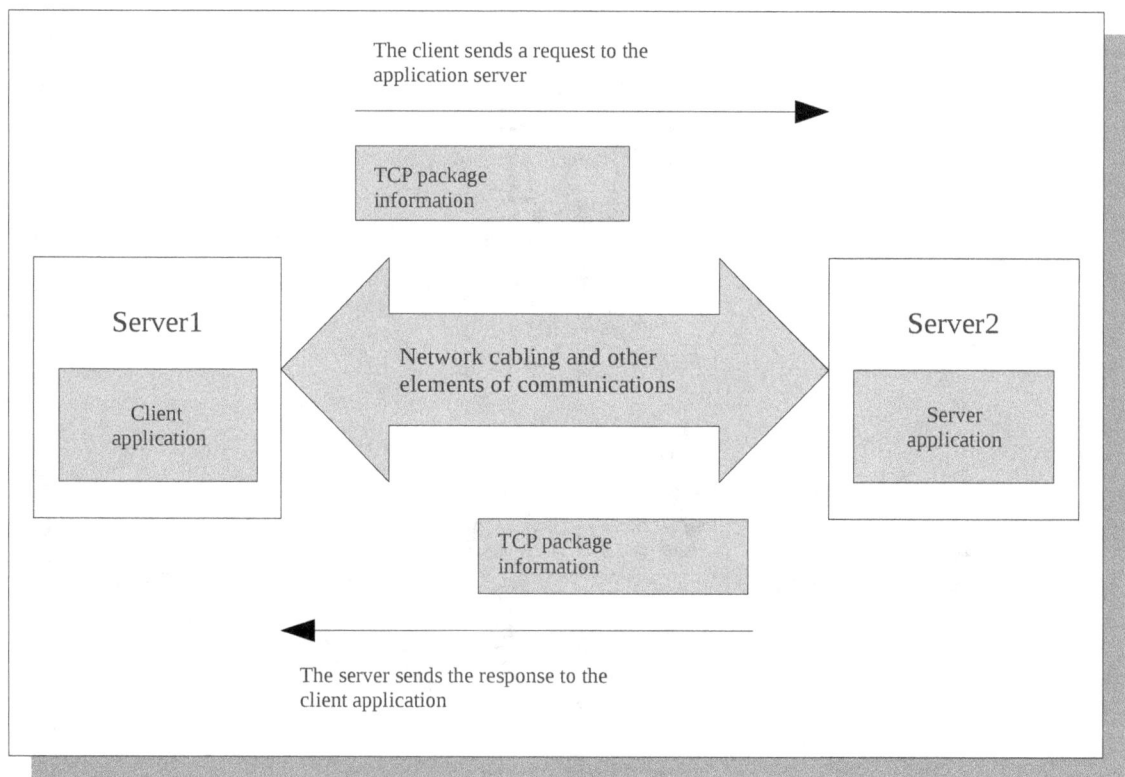

Server1 and *Server2* have a unique IP address and make sending and receiving, according to the task you have to do. The information that is sent is TCP packet and,

the channel, are the elements of communications.

In real life we have many examples of the use of this technology. For example, when we go to an ATM to withdraw money, we see an application with different options, such as consulting the balance or withdraw money. This is the client application that resides in all of all ATMs but by itself it would be useless. Need a central application to interpret our requests, this is, when we got to the last step in the process of withdrawing money, the application that resides in the ATM informs the application server that is responsible for carrying out the necessary validations (review in the database if there is sufficient balance, if you have not asked for a sum of money greater than the maximum allowed, etc.). The application server will send the validation code corresponding to the client application to show us an error code or will give us the money.

In order to continue to enter in the world of communications, we will explain some more technical concepts that have to be clear:

IP

It is a unique address of a system to ensure that it can be located within a network. Today, the most widespread version of this protocol is IPv4 and is based on 32-bit address, which causes the number of devices coming out on the market capable of connecting to the Internet, is straining the maximum number of IPs available. For this reason there is already the IPv6 protocol, based on 128-bit addresses.

One type of IP IPv4 is represented by four digits ranging from 0 to 255 separated by periods, such as: 192.168.1.2.

Each quartet is the decimal representation of a binary number. If we make the conversion of binary decimal number 255 we will see their value is equal to 11111111, this is, each quartet is eight bits, therefore, an IP address based on IPv4 consists of thirty-two bits, as commented previously (192.168.1.2 = 11000000.10101000.00000001.00000010).

The maximum number of IPs IPv4 is: 256 256 to the power of 4 = 4294967296
The maximum number of IPs IPv6 is: 4294967295 256 to the power of 4 = 340282366604025813516997721482669850625

Netmask

It is made up of four groups of eight bits each used to create subnetworks and know if a package must be sent within or outside the local network. The class A networks are the type Octet.X.X.X, for example, 192.X.X.X, where "X" are values ranging from 0 to 255. The Class B networks are represented by 192.168.X.X and class C by 192.168.1.X, this is, the class A networks will consist of a maximum 16777216 IPs (256 to the power of 3), the Class B may allocate 65,536 IPs (256 to the power of 2) and Class C may take up to 256 IPs.

To set up a network of class A, the multiplication of the binary IP by the mask must leave to 1 the first octet (for example: 11111111.00000000.00000000.00000000). A network of Class B will have the first 16-bit to 1 and, finally, a network of class C, will have the first 24-bit to 1 behind the logic multiplication. Remember that the binary multiplication is done bit by bit.

Example:

Based on the IP 192.168.1.2:

> Belong to a network of class A if its network mask is: 255.0.0.0

  The logical multiplication is:

    11000000.10101000.00000001.00000010
    11111111.00000000.00000000.00000000

    11111111.10101000.00000001.00000010

> Belong to a network of class B if its network mask is: 255.255.0.0

  The logical multiplication is:

    11000000.10101000.00000001.00000010
    11111111.11111111.00000000.00000000

    11111111.11111111.00000001.00000010

> Belong to a network of class C if its network mask is: 255.255.255.0

The logical multiplication is:

```
11000000.10101000.00000001.00000010
11111111.11111111.11111111.00000000
---------------------------------------------------
11111111.11111111.11111111.00000010
```

Following is a table representing mask network under Ipv4:

Binary	Decimal	CIDR
11111111.11111111.11111111.11111111	255.255.255.255	/32
11111111.11111111.11111111.11111110	255.255.255.254	/31
11111111.11111111.11111111.11111100	255.255.255.252	/30
11111111.11111111.11111111.11111000	255.255.255.248	/29
11111111.11111111.11111111.11110000	255.255.255.240	/28
11111111.11111111.11111111.11100000	255.255.255.224	/27
11111111.11111111.11111111.11000000	255.255.255.192	/26
11111111.11111111.11111111.10000000	255.255.255.128	/25
11111111.11111111.11111111.00000000	255.255.255.0	/24
11111111.11111111.11111110.00000000	255.255.254.0	/23
11111111.11111111.11111100.00000000	255.255.252.0	/22
11111111.11111111.11111000.00000000	255.255.248.0	/21
11111111.11111111.11110000.00000000	255.255.240.0	/20
11111111.11111111.11100000.00000000	255.255.224.0	/19
11111111.11111111.11000000.00000000	255.255.192.0	/18
11111111.11111111.10000000.00000000	255.255.128.0	/17

11111111.11111111.00000000.00000000	255.255.0.0	/16
11111111.11111110.00000000.00000000	255.254.0.0	/15
11111111.11111100.00000000.00000000	255.252.0.0	/14
11111111.11111000.00000000.00000000	255.248.0.0	/13
11111111.11110000.00000000.00000000	255.240.0.0	/12
11111111.11100000.00000000.00000000	255.224.0.0	/11
11111111.11000000.00000000.00000000	255.192.0.0	/10
11111111.10000000.00000000.00000000	255.128.0.0	/9
11111111.00000000.00000000.00000000	255.0.0.0	/8
11111110.00000000.00000000.00000000	254.0.0.0	/7
11111100.00000000.00000000.00000000	252.0.0.0	/6
11111000.00000000.00000000.00000000	248.0.0.0	/5
11110000.00000000.00000000.00000000	240.0.0.0	/4
11100000.00000000.00000000.00000000	224.0.0.0	/3
11000000.00000000.00000000.00000000	192.0.0.0	/2
10000000.00000000.00000000.00000000	128.0.0.0	/1
00000000.00000000.00000000.00000000	0.0.0.0	/0

IP addresses in the IPv6 protocol are represented in a different way as we see in IPV4. As IPV6 covers a much larger number of IPs in the RFC 2373 and RFC 2374 of 2003, was decided that these IPs are represented with eight bytes of four hexadecimal digit, so what gives us a 128-bit IP length. Therefore, the following IP address would be valid in the IPV6 protocol:

AB5 1503:4: 8FD4: 3DF1: 2ED3: AA21: 1357:1143

Broadcast addresses

IPs are being used to send a packet of information to all systems at once instead of sending a single package to each of them.

The broadcast IP is represented:

> In a class A network: Octet.255.255.255
> In a class B network: Octet.Octet.255.255
> In a class C network: Octet.Octet.Octet.255

Domain Name Server (DNS)

It contains a correlation table between the IP address and its name written in letters and numbers, this is, an IP address can be associated with a name.

For example, when we type the URL http://www.misgastos.net in our browser, we really are entering a numeric IP address because the DNS is responsible for the conversion. This is done well because for the humans is easier to remember a name that not a lot of numbers.

Example:

If we do not have any DNS configured, we can use the file */etc/hosts*:

```
[root@noname00 ~]# cat /etc/hosts
# Do not remove the following line, or various programs
# that require network functionality will fail.
# [ipaddress] [longname] [shortname]

# Local network
127.0.0.1       localhost.localdomain localhost
::1             localhost6.localdomain6 localhost6
192.168.1.2     noname00.casita.es noname00
192.168.1.5     vmnoname00. vmnoname00

# Remote network
130.177.169.84 TC79551
[root@noname00 ~]#
```

Gateway

It is an IP configured on a server able to connect to an external network, such as the Internet. The rest of the LAN systems will have to use this IP to communicate with servers in other networks.

Loopback IP

It is a local IP that is used to identify the own device, diagnose problems in the network card or indicate that the fate of a package is our own server.

This IP is represented as 127.0.0.1.

Dynamic Host Configuration Protocol (DHCP)

It is a client-server network protocol, which is used to obtain the parameters of network configuration, automatically.

MAC Address

It is the physical address of the network card. This address is unique for each device and is written directly on the hardware. Each manufacturer has its own identifier. This address is used to identify physically a hardware and create traffic rules specifically for it.

Communications port

It serves to establish communication with a service that is running on the system, either of a local or remote computer, via the network. When we want to connect to a computer or a client-server application, we need to know which service we must to use (ssh, telnet, http, ftp, sftp, mail entry, exit, proxy ...). Each service is associated to a port through which listens and must be unique for each application system. Therefore, besides to know the IP, we need to know the port to establish a communication.

For example, when we connect to a Web page with the browser, we are using port 80, which corresponds to the HTTP protocol, that is, it's the same type http://www.misgastos.net, which http://www.misgastos.net:80, however, system administrators reserve the right to change the default port in order to protect a service of a malicious attack.

There are 65535 ports available. 0 to 1024 are reserved for the TCP/UDP protocol, and the 1024 onwards for user applications. Some of the ports more used are:

Port/protocol	Description
9/tcp	Discard protocol. Removes any data it receives
9/udp	Discard protocol. Removes any data it receives
13/tcp	Daytime protocol. Current date
19/tcp	Chargen protocol. Character generator
19/udp	Chargen protocol. Character generator
20/tcp	FTP - data
21/tcp	FTP - control
22/tcp	SSH, SFTP y SFTP
23/tcp	Telnet
25/tcp	Simple Mail Transfer Protocol (SMTP)
37/tcp	Time
53/tcp	DNS
53/udp	DNS
69/udp	Trivial File Transfer Protocol (TFTP)
70/tcp	Gopher
79/tcp	Finger
80/tcp	HyperText Transfer Protocol (HTTP)
88/tcp	Kerberos - Agent authentication
110/tcp	Post Office Protocol (POP3)
123/udp	NTP Time synchronization protocol
123/tcp	NTP Time synchronization protocol
137/tcp	NetBIOS Name service
137/udp	NetBIOS Name service
138/tcp	NetBIOS Datagram Service
138/udp	NetBIOS Datagram Service
139/tcp	NetBIOS Sessions service
139/udp	NetBIOS Sessions service
143/tcp	Internet Message Access Protocol (IMAP4)

161/tcp	Simple Network Management Protocol (SNMP)
161/udp	Simple Network Management Protocol (SNMP)
162/tcp	SNMP-trap
162/udp	SNMP-trap
177/tcp	XDMCP – X11 Display manager
177/udp	XDMCP – X11 Display manager
389/tcp	LDAP
389/udp	LDAP
443/tcp	HTTPS
500/udp	IPSec ISAKMP, Local Security Authority
512/tcp	exec
513/tcp	login
514/udp	syslog – used for system logs
631/tcp	CUPS – printing system for UNIX
993/tcp	IMAP4 over SSL
995/tcp	POP3 over SSL
2049/tcp	NFSHTTP used by web caches and, by default, in squid cache
3128/tcp	HTTP used by web caches and, by default, in squid cache
6000/tcp	X11 used in X-windows

In the /etc/services can be consulted more ports and protocols associated with the different services.

Network configuration on a UNIX system

For example, if our communications manager gives us the following information for our system is able to go out to the Internet:

- **IP:** 192.168.1.2
- **Netmask:** 255.255.255.0
- **Broadcast:** 192.168.1.255
- **Gateway:** 192.168.1.1
- **Primary DNS:** 62.36.225.150
- **Secondary DNS:** 62.37.228.20

And in our system we see that we have the network interface *eth1*, after checking with the *ifconfig* command.

Configure a network card

Each UNIX system has its own method to configure network cards. For example, in HP-UX we will use SMH (or SAM) or we will edit the netconf file. In the case of Linux, we will use ifconfig or we will edit its configuration file. As already commented throughout the book, what interests us is the concept or know what to do, so every system administrator must know what commands to use.

To configure a network card with ifconfig, we will execute it as *root*:

    ifconfig eth1 192.168.1.2 netmask 255.255.255.0 broadcast 192.168.1.255 up

Now we see that the interface has been configured correctly:

```
[root@noname00 ~]# ifconfig eth1
eth1      Link encap:Ethernet  HWaddr 00:18:F3:64:59:CD
          inet addr:192.168.1.2  Bcast:192.168.1.255  Mask:255.255.255.0
          inet6 addr: fe80::218:f3ff:fe64:59cd/64 Scope:Link
          UP BROADCAST RUNNING PROMISC MULTICAST  MTU:1500  Metric:1
          RX packets:10839 errors:0 dropped:0 overruns:0 frame:0
```

```
          TX packets:10400 errors:0 dropped:0 overruns:0 carrier:0
          collisions:0 txqueuelen:1000
          RX bytes:1833596 (1.7 MiB)  TX bytes:1154964 (1.1 MiB)
          Interrupt:16

     [root@noname00 ~]#
```

As we can see, with this command, we see the MAC Address (HWAddr), the IP assigned to the interface, the broadcast IP, network mask, if the network is up and if errors are occurring.

In systems where switches are involved, the switch admistrador must to tell us how fast we have to configure the network card (10, 100, 1000, full or half duplex).
Depending on the operating system and driver network card, we will use a command or another.

- Example to see the speed on HP-UX:

    [root@noname00 ~]# lanadmin -x 0
    Speed = 100 Full-Duplex.
    Autonegotiation = Off.
    [root@noname00 ~]#

- Example to see the speed on Linux:

    [root@noname00 ~]# ethtool eth0
    Settings for eth0:
        Supported ports: [TP MII]
        Supported link modes: 10baseT/Half 10baseT/Full
                                100baseT/Half 100baseT/Full
        Supports auto-negotiation: Yes
        Advertised link modes: 10baseT/Half 10baseT/Full
                                100baseT/Half 100baseT/Full

        Advertised auto-negotiation: Yes
        Speed: 100Mb/s
        Duplex: Full
        Port: Twisted Pair
        PHYAD: 1

>   *Transceiver: internal*
>   *Auto-negotiation: on*
>   *Supports Wake-on: puag*
>   *Wake-on: g*
>   *Link detected: yes*

- Example to see the speed on (with a different network card driver):

    [root@noname00 ~]# mii-tool eth1
    eth1: no autonegotiation, 10baseT-HD, link ok

Gateway configuration

Taking as example the command that is used on a Linux RedHat:
    route add default gw 192.168.1.1

Once executed the previous instruction, we can see if it has been applied the settings:

```
[root@noname00 ~]# route
Kernel IP routing table
Destination     Gateway         Genmask         Flags Metric Ref    Use Iface
172.16.166.0    *               255.255.255.0   U     0      0        0 vmnet8
172.16.165.0    *               255.255.255.0   U     0      0        0 vmnet1
192.168.1.0     *               255.255.255.0   U     0      0        0 vmnet0
192.168.1.0     *               255.255.255.0   U     0      0        0 eth1
link-local      *               255.255.0.0     U     0      0        0 eth1
default         192.168.1.1     0.0.0.0         UG    0      0        0 vmnet0
[root@noname00 ~]#
```

DNS configuration

We will edit the file */etc/resolv.conf* with the DNS provided by the communications administrator, as follows:

    [root@noname00 ~]# cat /etc/resolv.conf
    nameserver 62.36.225.150

nameserver 62.37.228.20
[root@noname00 ~]#

Once completed these steps, we can go out to the Internet:

[root@noname00 ~]# ping www.misgastos.net
PING www.misgastos.net (91.186.20.106) 56(84) bytes of data.
64 bytes from 91.186.20.106: icmp_seq=1 ttl=53 time=67.2 ms
64 bytes from 91.186.20.106: icmp_seq=2 ttl=53 time=66.2 ms
64 bytes from 91.186.20.106: icmp_seq=3 ttl=53 time=66.6 ms
64 bytes from 91.186.20.106: icmp_seq=4 ttl=53 time=66.5 ms
^C
--- www.misgastos.net ping statistics ---
4 packets transmitted, 4 received, 0% packet loss, time 3435ms
rtt min/avg/max/mdev = 66.246/66.692/67.289/0.456 ms
[root@noname00 ~]# [root@noname00 ~]#

Virtual IP configuration

A network card can be assigned more than one IP. This is what is called virtual IP and serves to set up multiple applications or services by different IPs using the same physical network card. Each of the IPs can use the 65,535 available ports, and all must belong to the same network (because the network cabling does not change).

Then, we configure the virtual 192.168.1.10 IP in the network interface *eth1*:

[root@noname00 ~]# ifconfig eth1**:1** 192.168.1.10 netmask 255.255.255.0 broadcast 192.168.1.255 up

And we check the configuration:

[root@noname00 ~]# ifconfig
eth1   Link encap:Ethernet HWaddr 00:18:F3:64:59:CD
        inet addr:192.168.1.2 Bcast:192.168.1.255 Mask:255.255.255.0
        inet6 addr: fe80::218:f3ff:fe64:59cd/64 Scope:Link
        UP BROADCAST RUNNING PROMISC MULTICAST MTU:1500 Metric:1

```
          RX packets:20261 errors:0 dropped:0 overruns:0 frame:0
          TX packets:19108 errors:0 dropped:0 overruns:0 carrier:0
          collisions:0 txqueuelen:1000
          RX bytes:2454045 (2.3 MiB)  TX bytes:1746619 (1.6 MiB)
          Interrupt:16

eth1:1    Link encap:Ethernet  HWaddr 00:18:F3:64:59:CD
          inet addr:192.168.1.10  Bcast:192.168.1.255  Mask:255.255.255.0
          UP BROADCAST RUNNING PROMISC MULTICAST  MTU:1500  Metric:1
          Interrupt:16
```

```
[root@noname00 ~]# ping 192.168.1.10
PING 192.168.1.10 (192.168.1.10) 56(84) bytes of data.
64 bytes from 192.168.1.10: icmp_seq=1 ttl=64 time=0.039 ms
64 bytes from 192.168.1.10: icmp_seq=2 ttl=64 time=0.037 ms
64 bytes from 192.168.1.10: icmp_seq=3 ttl=64 time=0.038 ms
^C
--- 192.168.1.10 ping statistics ---
3 packets transmitted, 3 received, 0% packet loss, time 2342ms
rtt min/avg/max/mdev = 0.037/0.038/0.039/0.000 ms
[root@noname00 ~]#
```

At the first command *ifconfig*, it is necessary to highlight the name of the network card indicated: *eth1:1*. This means that we have set up the **first** virtual IP. If we would want to set up a **second**, we would use eth1:**2**, and so on. Also note that the MAC Address coincides on both network interfaces (physical and virtual).

Delete the configuration of a network interface

- We stop the interface:

    ```
    [root@noname00 ~]# ifconfig eth1:1 down
    ```

- We remove it:

    If this is a physical interface, that is, not virtual, we will place in the directory

/etc/sysconfig/network-scripts, we will remove the configuration file associated, for example, *ifcfg-eth1*, and we will restart the network services with the command of RedHat: *service network restart*.

Configuring an interface *bridge*

An interface *bridge* is a link between two network interfaces that may belong to different networks. This system makes possible that a server of a network may communicate with a server of another network as is both servers belong to the same.

Imagine a BSD UNIX system with two network cards. One of them uses RJ45 wiring and the other optical fiber. Both cards are configured with different networks and we want to make a bridge between them. The first interface responds to the name of *ep0*, while the second is called *fxp0*. To make the bridge, we will edit the file *bridgename.bridbge0*, as follows:

```
[root@noname00 ~]# cat brid gename.bridge0
add fxp0
add ep0
up
[root@noname00 ~]#
```

and we will restart the network services with the command */etc/netstart*.

Now that it is beginning to virtualize systems of type VMWare, VirtualBox or Integrity Virtual Machines, to name some, this kind of connection can be helpful to connect a virtual server system with its system "father". We will use a RedHat Linux, an interface typical of VMWare (vmnet0), a system interface (eth1) and the *bridge-utils* software for configuring the bridge. We will do as follows:

```
[root@noname00 /]# cat /etc/init.d/creabridge

# Configuration of the "Bridge" interface

# Declaring the interface bridge
brctl addbr br0
```

```
# Added interfaces that form part of the bridge
brctl addif br0 vmnet0
brctl addif br0 eth1

brctl setageing vmnet0 0
brctl sethello vmnet0 30
brctl setmaxage vmnet0 180
ifconfig br0 192.168.1.3 netmask 255.255.255.0 up

# Restart the network services to apply the change.

service network restart
[root@noname00 /]#
```

ARP tables

ARP tables contain the relationship between the MAC address and the logical IP.

```
[noname00]root:/root # arp -a
172.23.65.1 (172.23.65.1) at 0:0:5e:0:1:1 ether
7.1.2.6 (7.1.2.6) at 40:0:22:22:c6:7c rif - ieee802.5
7.1.1.4 (7.1.1.4) at 0:8:de:1:63:66 rif - ieee802.5
7.1.1.1 (7.1.1.1) at 0:50:d1:32:a:38 rif - ieee802.5
172.27.1.131 (172.27.1.131) -- no entry
172.23.84.183 (172.23.84.183) at 0:4:23:a7:19:72 ether
10.242.230.129 (10.242.230.129) -- no entry
172.27.1.5 (172.27.1.5) -- no entry
lan_console (172.23.65.16) at 0:30:6e:4b:c9:e7 ether
172.23.65.2 (172.23.65.2) at 0:2:85:27:3f:20 ether
10.240.1.1 (10.240.1.1) -- no entry
[noname00]root:/root #
```

For the physical addresses can connect with the logic addresses, the ARP protocol questions to all computers on the network their physical addresses, launching a call to the broadcast IP. Then stores in the cache a relationship between the MAC and IP Address numbers in order to speed up translation.

When a network card is replaced, all devices that make up the network, such as a router, take a while to refresh its own ARP table. If we want to force the refresh, we can delete the entries that we are interested in our system and then test a connection to the affected IPs. Would be as follows:

```
arp -d 172.23.65.1
ping 172.23.65.1
```

Other commands system linked to computer networks

ping

Tests the connectivity from our system to an IP. It uses the signal 8 of the ICMP protocol.

```
[root@noname00 ~]# ping www.misgastos.net
PING www.misgastos.net (91.186.20.106) 56(84) bytes of data.
64 bytes from 91.186.20.106: icmp_seq=1 ttl=53 time=65.0 ms
64 bytes from 91.186.20.106: icmp_seq=2 ttl=53 time=65.9 ms
64 bytes from 91.186.20.106: icmp_seq=3 ttl=53 time=66.4 ms
64 bytes from 91.186.20.106: icmp_seq=4 ttl=53 time=64.5 ms
64 bytes from 91.186.20.106: icmp_seq=5 ttl=53 time=67.2 ms
64 bytes from 91.186.20.106: icmp_seq=6 ttl=53 time=67.4 ms
64 bytes from 91.186.20.106: icmp_seq=7 ttl=53 time=65.8 ms
^C
--- www.misgastos.net ping statistics ---
7 packets transmitted, 7 received, 0% packet loss, time 6396ms
rtt min/avg/max/mdev = 64.529/66.075/67.453/1.005 ms
[root@noname00 ~]#
```

traceroute

Shows the path connecting that we follow until connecting with the IP destination:

```
[root@noname00 ~]# traceroute www.google.com
```

```
traceroute to www.google.com (64.233.169.99), 64 hops max, 40 byte packets
 1  * * *
 2  172.16.183.1 (172.16.183.1)  23 ms  23 ms  22 ms
 3  10.127.66.229 (10.127.66.229) [MPLS: Label 1479 Exp 0]  38 ms  51 ms  38 ms
 4  cnt-00-tge1-0-0.gw.cantv.net (200.44.43.85)  38 ms  38 ms  37 ms
 5  cri-00-pos1-0-0.border.cantv.net (200.44.43.50)  51 ms  43 ms  43 ms
 6  sl-st21-mia-14-1-0.sprintlink.net (144.223.245.233)  94 ms  93 ms  93 ms
 7  sl-bb20-mia-5-0-0.sprintlink.net (144.232.9.198)  95 ms  93 ms  93 ms
 8  sl-crs1-mia-0-4-0-0.sprintlink.net (144.232.2.248)  94 ms  95 ms  95 ms
 9  sl-crs1-atl-0-0-0-1.sprintlink.net (144.232.20.48)  104 ms  104 ms  103 ms
10  sl-st20-atl-1-0-0.sprintlink.net (144.232.18.133)  104 ms  103 ms  *
11  144.223.47.234 (144.223.47.234)  103 ms  103 ms  103 ms
12  64.233.174.86 (64.233.174.86)  98 ms  97 ms 64.233.174.84 (64.233.174.84)  103 ms
13  216.239.48.68 (216.239.48.68)  105 ms  104 ms  106 ms
14  72.14.236.200 (72.14.236.200)  106 ms *  105 ms
15  72.14.232.21 (72.14.232.21)  110 ms  109 ms  107 ms
16  * yo-in-f99.google.com (64.233.169.99)  100 ms  99 ms
```

netstat

It gives us information on active connections in our system. If we query the help of the command by *man*, we can see the combinations of different parameters that exist to get the information we are interested. Next, are attached some examples:

We see the top 15 active connections:

```
[root@noname00 ~]# netstat |head -15
Active Internet connections (w/o servers)
Proto Recv-Q Send-Q Local Address           Foreign Address         State
Active UNIX domain sockets (w/o servers)
Proto RefCnt Flags     Type       State         I-Node Path
unix  2      [ ]       DGRAM                    396    @/com/ubuntu/upstart
unix  2      [ ]       DGRAM                    712    @/org/kernel/udev/udevd
```

```
unix  4    [ ]       DGRAM              21647  /dev/log
unix  2    [ ]       DGRAM               6249  @/org/freedesktop/hal/udev_event
unix  3    [ ]       STREAM   CONNECTED  23168  /tmp/.esd-500/socket
unix  3    [ ]       STREAM   CONNECTED  23167
unix  3    [ ]       STREAM   CONNECTED  23159  /var/run/dbus/system_bus_socket
unix  3    [ ]       STREAM   CONNECTED  23158
unix  3    [ ]       STREAM   CONNECTED  23152  /tmp/orbit-David/linc-189e-0-211a568b80254
unix  3    [ ]       STREAM   CONNECTED  23151
unix  3    [ ]       STREAM   CONNECTED  23149  /tmp/orbit-David/linc-100c-0-5e19795a49f80
[root@noname00 ~]#
```

We get information about network interfaces:

```
[root@noname00 ~]# netstat -ni
Kernel Interface table
Iface    MTU Met   RX-OK RX-ERR RX-DRP RX-OVR    TX-OK TX-ERR TX-DRP TX-OVR Flg
eth1    1500  0    35906   0    0     0         30333   0    0      0 BMPRU
lo     16436  0     2900   0    0     0          2900   0    0      0 LRU
vmnet0  1500  0    30876   0    0     0         30295   0    0      0 BMRU
vmnet1  1500  0        0   0    0     0            27   0    0      0 BMRU
vmnet8  1500  0        0   0    0     0            27   0    0      0 BMRU
[root@noname00 ~]#
```

We see the first 15 active connections with the communications protocol used, the port and the state:

```
[root@noname00 ~]# netstat -an |head -15
Active Internet connections (servers and established)
Proto Recv-Q Send-Q Local Address        Foreign Address       State
tcp     0     0 0.0.0.0:902              0.0.0.0:*             LISTEN
tcp     0     0 0.0.0.0:43338            0.0.0.0:*             LISTEN
tcp     0     0 0.0.0.0:8333             0.0.0.0:*             LISTEN
tcp     0     0 0.0.0.0:111              0.0.0.0:*             LISTEN
tcp     0     0 127.0.0.1:8307           0.0.0.0:*             LISTEN
tcp     0     0 0.0.0.0:22               0.0.0.0:*             LISTEN
tcp     0     0 127.0.0.1:631            0.0.0.0:*             LISTEN
```

```
tcp    0    0 0.0.0.0:25          0.0.0.0:*         LISTEN
tcp    0    0 0.0.0.0:8222        0.0.0.0:*         LISTEN
tcp    0    0 ::ffff:127.0.0.1:8005   :::*          LISTEN
tcp    0    0 :::8009             :::*              LISTEN
tcp    0    0 :::139              :::*              LISTEN
tcp    0    0 :::14029            :::*              LISTEN
```
[root@noname00 ~]#

We get the routing table:

```
[root@noname00 ~]# netstat -nr
Kernel IP routing table
Destination     Gateway         Genmask         Flags   MSS Window  irtt Iface
172.16.166.0    0.0.0.0         255.255.255.0   U       0 0         0 vmnet8
172.16.165.0    0.0.0.0         255.255.255.0   U       0 0         0 vmnet1
192.168.1.0     0.0.0.0         255.255.255.0   U       0 0         0 vmnet0
192.168.1.0     0.0.0.0         255.255.255.0   U       0 0         0 eth1
169.254.0.0     0.0.0.0         255.255.0.0     U       0 0         0 eth1
0.0.0.0         192.168.1.1     0.0.0.0         UG      0 0         0 vmnet0
```
[root@noname00 ~]#

According to the version of netstat that we have, the information obtained by the parameters may vary.

hostname

Displays the name of our system.

```
[root@noname00 ~]# hostname
noname00
[root@noname00 ~]#
```

Each UNIX can have its own configuration file to store this information. For example, in a RedHat is saved in:

```
[root@noname00 etc]# more /etc/sysconfig/network
NETWORKING=yes
HOSTNAME=noname00
```

>   DOMAINNAME=casita.es
>   IPV6_DEFAULTGW=
>   [root@noname00 etc]#

Or in an HP-UX system can use the command *set_parms*:

>   [stsint1] root:/etc # set_parms
>   Usage: set_parms <argument>
>   Where <argument> can be:
>   hostname
>   timezone → The time zone is stored in the environment variable $TZ
>   date_time
>   root_passwd
>   ip_address
>   addl_netwrk
>   or initial (for entire initial boot-time dialog sequence)

Each administrator system, should documented according to the version of UNIX that is using.

domainname

Displays the domain name that belongs our system. A domain is a common name used to group a set of servers. For example, the servers that make up a web page could have the following philosophy:

>   Webserver1.myweb.com
>   Webserver2.myweb.com
>   Applicationserver1.myweb.com
>   Applicationserver2.myweb.com
>   BBDD1.myweb.com
>   BBDD2.myweb.com

The first two systems makes the role of Web servers using the Apache software. The next two contain the application we use at the website, written in Java and configured in high availability through the application server Weblogic. The last two have installed Oracle database that requires the application to store or retrieve information. Each of the servers that are part of the service have their own IP, operating system and other specific configurations, but all belong to a common domain: myweb.com.

To prevent two different entities use the same name in the public domain on the Internet, there are global organizations responsible for managing both the range of IP addresses as domain names that can use every entity, either a country, a company, a region, or a particular.

nslookup

Shows the relationship between IP and its name.

    [root@noname00 sysconfig]# nslookup www.misgastos.net
    Server: 62.36.225.150
    Address: 62.36.225.150#53
    Non-authoritative answer:
    Name: www.misgastos.net
    Address: 91.186.20.106

    [root@noname00 sysconfig]#

telnet

Logs in a remote system. The most commonly used syntax is:

    telnet IP port

ssh

Log in encrypted on a remote system. We can use as:

    ssh user@IP

Later we will go into more detail on the operation and configuration of the encrypted connections.

finger

It gives us information about users connected to the same network.

```
[root@noname00]# finger user1
Login: user1                        Name: user1
Directory: /home/user1              Shell: /bin/bash
On since lun nov 24 18:55 (CET) on tty7 from :0
On since lun nov 24 19:16 (CET) on pts/0 from :0.0
On since lun nov 24 20:11 (CET) on pts/1 from :0.0
   14 seconds idle
No mail.
No Plan.
[root@noname00]#
```

talk

It serves to initiate a conversation with another user connected to the same network. It is one of the first chat programs that exist.

rpcinfo

Gives a list of all programs that are making use of the RPC daemon (Remote Call Procedure). This service is for an application can execute code on a remote system.

```
[root@noname00 ~]# rpcinfo
  program version netid   address              service   owner
   100000   4     tcp     0.0.0.0.0.111        portmapper superuser
   100000   3     tcp     0.0.0.0.0.111        portmapper superuser
   100000   2     tcp     0.0.0.0.0.111        portmapper superuser
   100000   4     udp     0.0.0.0.0.111        portmapper superuser
   100000   3     udp     0.0.0.0.0.111        portmapper superuser
   100000   2     udp     0.0.0.0.0.111        portmapper superuser
   100000   4     local   /var/run/rpcbind.sock portmapper superuser
   100000   3     local   /var/run/rpcbind.sock portmapper superuser
   100000   2     local   /var/run/rpcbind.sock portmapper superuser
   100024   1     udp     0.0.0.0.25.159       status    unknown
   100024   1     tcp     0.0.0.0.169.74       status    unknown
```

The proxy *squid*

Concepts

A proxy is a server that separates two different networks. Its functions include:

- Centralizing traffic between two networks.
- Accelerate access to Web content through a cache.
- Restrict certain types of traffic according to the rules set out in its configuration file.
- Allow access to other networks, like the Internet, to servers located in a private network.
- Store a log of network traffic.

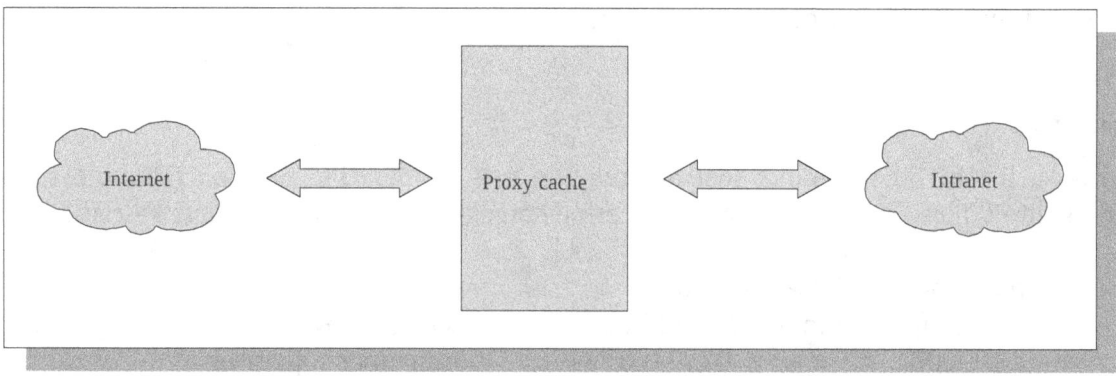

For example, if we have a server in a protected network without an Internet connection, and we have found a vulnerability in an application that must connect to the Internet, by an own online update tool, to download a patch that fixes the security hole. In this case, the application server can use a proxy to connect to Internet and download the software it needs.

As mentioned earlier, a proxy can serve to accelerate the loading of Web pages. This is achieved by using cache memory. In this type of memory are stored data from other previous requests in order to avoid having to connect to the original Web page to download a required data. As the information is stored locally the access to this data is very fast and, therefore, the web page loads faster and the traffic going through the network is reduced. When the data needed for a Web page is newer than the stored in the cache, it is necessary to connect to the original page.

squid is a free software under GPL license, widely used in the Unix world that takes several years to develop. The official website is http://www.squid-cache.org/

squid configuration

The configuration file of this proxy, generally, is on the path */etc/squid/squid.conf*. Here are some of their most useful parameters:

- **visible_hostname** *Name:* The proxy will have its own hostname.
- **cache_effective_user** *proxy* and **cache_effective_group** proxy: Defines the user group that will administer the proxy system. In this case, both the user and the group called *proxy*.
- **http_port:** Establishes the communications port to be used by squid. We can also force an IP exclusive use.

    http_port 3128
    http_port 192.168.1.2:3128

- **dns_nameservers:** Fixes DNS servers that will use the proxy.

    dns_nameservers 7.2.1.144

- **cache_mem 120 MB:** Setting the amount of physical memory allocated to the cache.
- **cache_dir:** Configures disk space for the cache.

    Example:

    cache_dir ufs /var/spool/squid 100 15 150

    We just allocate 100MB of disk, allowing 15 first-level directories and 150 of a second.

- acl [list_name] src [list_components]: This option is used to allow access to the proxy to some servers of the private network. In the *src* parameter is indicated the IPs which have access.

    Example:

    acl MyNetwork src 130.177.169.0 localhost 172.23.2.137

    We can also create rules to deny access to certain servers of the external network:

    acl web_denieds dstdomain .sex.com

    We can also limit the connection ports:

    acl SSL_ports port 443 445
    acl CONNECT method CONNECT
    http_access deny !SSL_ports
    http_access deny CONNECT !SSL_ports

    In this case we've created a list called *SSL_ports* that allows connection to ports 443 and 445 through the *CONNECT* method.

    We can set up schedules of connection:

    acl IP_allowed src 192.168.1.2 192.168.1.3
    acl shedule time MTWHF 8:00-18:00 working hours
    acl servdor1 src 192.168.1.25
    acl mañana time 8:00-13:00

- **http_access:** It specifies the IPs to allow or deny the use of squid.

    http_access allow MyNetwork !IPs_denied

    If within the IPs grouped in MyNetwork there are some who want to deny the use, we will put the symbol "!" before the IPs which interests us.

- cache_mgr email: We define an e-mail address to which we are reporting problems with the cache.
- **httpd_accel_host** *servidor***:** The server is configured to be accelerating, that is,

in the case of a web page, if the original has not been changed with respect to data stored in the cache, this data will be obtained from the cache, not from the original server to obtain a charging time of the page faster. With *httpd_accel_host virtual*, we indicated that we want to accelerate more than one server.

Startup *squid*

The first time that is started, has run the command squid-z to create the directory structure, then we will can use */etc/rc.d/init.d/squid {start|stop|reload|force-reload|restart}*.

To test the proper functioning of the proxy, we will execute the command squidclient http://www.misgastos.net or we will configure our browser to the IP and port that we have pre-configured:

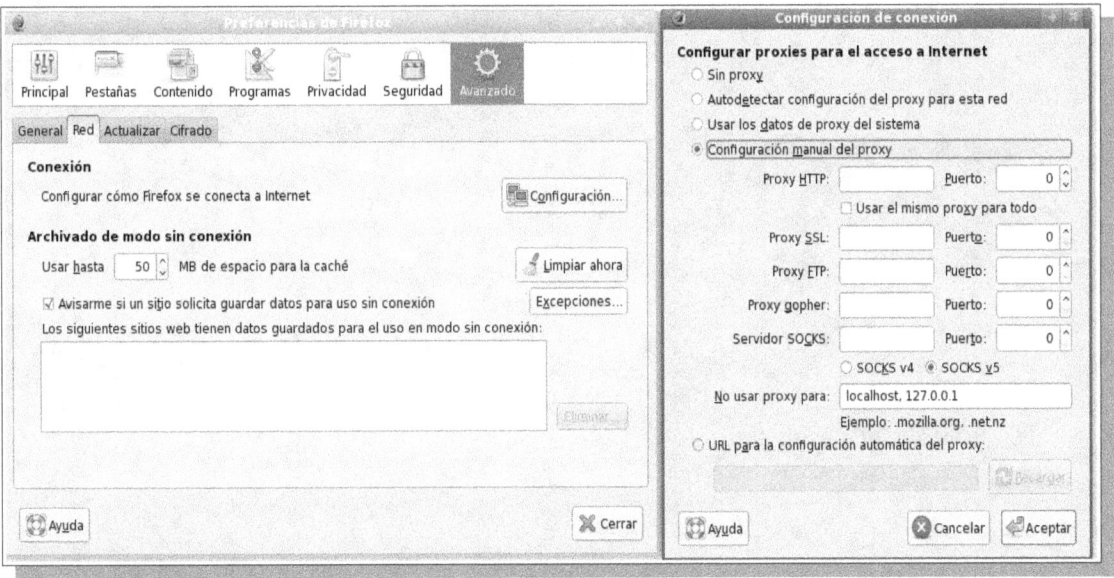

A simple example configuration:

    visible_hostname noname00.com

```
dns_testnames localhost

http_port 3128
cache_effective_user sqdadm

cache_access_log /etc/squid/logs/access.log
cache_log /etc/squid/logs/cache.log
cache_store_log /etc/squid/logs/store.log
pid_filename /etc/logs/squid.pid

cache_dir ufs /etc/squid/cache 100 16 256
coredump_dir /etc/squid/cache

acl All src 0/0
acl MyNetwork src 130.177.169.0 localhost 172.23.2.137

http_access allow MyNetwork
http_access deny All
```

File Transfer Protocol (FTP)

Concepts

It is a communications protocol used to transfer files across the network, making use of the concept client-server for the communications between applications. The client connects to the server, it authenticates with a username and password and we can send and receive files. Below is an example of connection:

```
[root@noname00 ~]# ftp misgastos.net
Connected to misgastos.net (91.186.20.106).
220 ProFTPD 1.2.10 Server (sc12.co.uk) [91.186.20.106]
Name (misgastos.net:user1): user1
331 Password required for user1.
Password:
230 User user1 logged in.
Remote system type is UNIX.
Using binary mode to transfer files.
ftp>
```

Once login, we can type the FTP commands that we need:

Command	Function
!	Executes a command from the local operating system
$	Executes a macro
?/help	Displays help
account	Sends a command to the account of the remote server
append	Concatenates a file

ASCII	The transfer is for ASCII files
bell	It sounds a bell when the command has been completed
binary	The transfer is for binary file
bye	The session is ended
case	Mapping the same letters
cd	Entering or leaving a directory
cdup	Come to the parent directory on the remote server
chmod	Changing permissions on the remote server
close	Finish the FTP session
cr	Carriage return
delete	Deleting a file on the remote server
dir/ls	We see the content of the remote directory
disconnect	Finish the FTP session
get	Copy a file from the remote server to the local system
hash	Is printed on the screen the "#" for each buffer transferred
lcd	We changed the directory for the local system
macdef	Define a macro
mdelete	We delete several files
mdir/mls	List the contents of multiple remote directories
mget	Receives more files
mkdir	Create a directory on the remote machine
mode	Sets the transfer mode
modetime	Clock mode
mput	Send multiple files from the local to remote directory
newer	Receives the remote file if it is newer than that of the local machine
nlist	List the contents of multiple remote directories
ntrans	Sets translation table for mapping file names

o/open	Opens a remote connection from the FTP shell
prompt	Force execution of multiple commands
proxy	Connecting alternative
put	Send a file to the remote system
pwd	Displays the working directory on the remote machine
quit	FTP session ends and leaves
recv	Receive file from remote machine
rstatus	Shows the status of the remote machine
rename	It renames a file name
reset	Clean the responses of queued commands
rmdir	Deletes a directory of the remote machine
send	Send a file to the remote server
site	Send a specific command to the remote machine
size	Shows the size of a file
status	Shows the local state
system	Shows the type of remote system
tenex	Transferring files of type Tenex
trace	Turns traces transfer packages
type	Sets the file type to transferred
user	Serves to authenticate again on the remote server
umask	Sets the permissions system in the remote side

Examples of the use of FTP commands

> We are placed in the local directory */root/scripts*:

ftp> lcd scripts
Local directory now /root/scripts

ftp>

> We look at the contents of the remote directory:

ftp> ls -la
227 Entering Passive Mode (91,186,20,106,211,213).
150 Opening ASCII mode data connection for file list
drwxr-xr-x 3 smtz   (?)   26 Aug 29 08:01 .
drwxr-xr-x 3 smtz   (?)   26 Aug 29 08:01 ..
drwxr-xr-x 11 smtz   (?)   4096 Sep 1 13:54 misgastos.net
226 Transfer complete.
ftp>

> We look at the contents of the local directory:

ftp> !ls -l
total 40544
-rwxr-xr-x 1 root root   493 abr 19 2008 backup_oracle_total.sh
-rw-r--r-- 1 root root 17725318 sep 27 20:30 backup_total2008-09-27.log
-rw-r--r-- 1 root root 1446620 oct 1 19:30 backup_total2008-10-01.log.gz
-rw-r--r-- 1 root root 1428323 oct 2 17:25 backup_total2008-10-02.log.gz
-rw-r--r-- 1 root root 1428420 oct 12 12:50 backup_total2008-10-12.log.gz
-rw-r--r-- 1 root root 17887201 oct 31 20:19 backup_total2008-10-31.log
-rw-r--r-- 1 root root 1495556 oct 31 18:59 backup_total2008-10-31.log.gz
-rwxr-xr-x 1 root root   1142 sep 27 22:32 backup_total.sh
-rwxr-xr-x 1 root root   517 abr 19 2008 backup_vmware.sh
-rwxr-xr-x 1 root root   195 sep 30 21:29 crea_bridge2.sh
-rwxr-xr-x 1 root root   174 sep 30 21:00 crea_bridge.sh
-rwxr-xr-x 1 root root   47 jul 12 21:58 start_mysql.sh
-rwxr-xr-x 1 root root   20 jun 29 09:01 stop_mysql.sh
ftp>

> We indicate that the file transfer is done in binary mode:

ftp> bin
200 Type set to I
ftp>

> We send the file "backup_total.sh":

ftp> put backup_total.sh
local: backup_total.sh remote: backup_total.sh
227 Entering Passive Mode (91,186,20,106,171,233).
150 Opening BINARY mode data connection for backup_total.sh
226 Transfer complete.
1142 bytes sent in 0,0181 secs (63,09 Kbytes/sec)
ftp>

➤ We check that the file has arrived:

ftp> ls -la
227 Entering Passive Mode (91,186,20,106,145,213).
150 Opening ASCII mode data connection for file list
drwxr-xr-x   3 smtz   (?)   48 Nov 25 15:20 .
drwxr-xr-x   3 smtz   (?)   48 Nov 25 15:20 ..
-rw-r--r--   1 smtz   (?)   1142 Nov 25 15:20 backup_total.sh
drwxr-xr-x 11 smtz   (?)   4096 Sep 1 13:54 misgastos.net
226 Transfer complete.
ftp>

➤ We rename the remote file:

ftp> rename backup_total.sh remote_backup_total.sh
350 File or directory exists, ready for destination name.
250 Rename successful
ftp>

ftp> ls -l
227 Entering Passive Mode (91,186,20,106,170,77).
150 Opening ASCII mode data connection for file list
drwxr-xr-x 11 smtz   (?)   4096 Sep 1 13:54 misgastos.net
-rw-r--r--   1 smtz   (?)   1142 Nov 25 15:20 remote_backup_total.sh
226 Transfer complete.
ftp>

➤ We download the file "remote_backup_total.sh" to our system:

ftp> mget remote_backup*
mget remote_backup_total.sh? y
227 Entering Passive Mode (91,186,20,106,224,44).

```
150 Opening BINARY mode data connection for remote_backup_total.sh (1142
bytes)
226 Transfer complete.
1142 bytes received in 0,0111 secs (103,11 Kbytes/sec)
ftp>

ftp> !ls -la rem*
-rw-r--r-- 1 root root 1142 nov 25 16:23 remote_backup_total.sh
ftp>
```

➢ We delete the file on the remote system:

```
ftp> delete remote_backup_total.sh
250 DELE command successful
ftp>

ftp> ls -l
227 Entering Passive Mode (91,186,20,106,197,143).
150 Opening ASCII mode data connection for file list
drwxr-xr-x  11 smtz     (?)          4096 Sep  1 13:54 misgastos.net
226 Transfer complete.
ftp>
```

➢ We leave of the FTP session:

```
ftp> bye
221 Goodbye.
[root@noname00 ~]#
```

FTP server configuration

We will configure the system for the service starts from the first moment that we have available the system. To do so will edit the file */etc/inetd.conf*. In some systems this file can be replaced for *xinetd.conf*.

```
[root@noname00 ~]# cat /etc/inetd.conf |grep ftpd
ftp       stream tcp6 nowait root /usr/lbin/ftpd    ftpd -l –a
```

The command *inetd -c* (or *xinetd -c*) reads the configuration file *(x)inetd.conf* and applies the changes without having to reboot the system.

Once we have activated the FTP server we must configure it according to our needs:

- File */etc/ftpd/ftpaccess*: Contains a multitude of parameters that define the operation of the FTP server. Set groups, limit the number of simultaneous connections or configure traces of transfers, are just some of the things that can be configured in this file. As always, support that shows the *man* command will be useful for us.

    Example configuration:

        [root@noname00 ~]# cat /etc/ftpd/ftpaccess
        # Transfers log in /var/adm/syslog/xferlog
        log transfers guest inbound,outbound

        # We define the class that contains real users and those defined as a guest. If a user is not here the connection can not be establish.

        class myc_all_local real,guest 172.* 130.177.169.* 192.168.2.*

        class myc_all__internet real,guest 213.172.44.100 213.172.44.98 213.172.44.99 62.151.16.230 195.77.57.105 217.126.114.44 194.30.12.44 192.148.167.122 172.23.2.75 82.144.100.54 80.37.182.184

        #The users of type guest are the group's ftpsgrp
        guestgroup ftpsgrp

        # When connecting to the server
        message /BIENVENIDA login

        # When changing directory
        message .message cwd=*

        # Copyright message
        banner /etc/motd

        # Only allow uploads on the directories with yes

```
upload /ftp/apl1 * no
upload /ftp/apl1 /incoming  yes user1 usergrp 0660 nodirs
upload /ftp/apl1 /incoming/inc1  yes user1 usergrp 0660 nodirs
upload /ftp/sis1 /incoming/inc2  yes user1 usergrp 0660 nodirs

[root@noname00 ~]#
```

- File */etc/ftpd/ftphosts*: Allows or denies access to certain FTP accounts from remote servers. The syntax of the file is the following:

    allow/deny *user* a*addrglob* [*addrglob*...]

    ```
    allow   ftp    10.0.0.*
    deny    ftpuser1   10.*.*.*
    allow   root   *
    ```

- File */etc/ftpd/ftpusers*: Restrict access to FTP users specified.

    ```
    [root@noname00 ~]# cat ftpusers
    root
    bin
    daemon
    adm
    lp
    sync
    shutdown
    halt
    mail
    news
    uucp
    nobody
    ```

Jail FTP users to their home directory

In a public FTP server does not interest us that anyone can get in to see the content of other system directories. It is simply an issue for our own safety and privacy of all users store their files on our server.

We can configure each FTP account so that it is jailed in a subdirectory of our system and can not go out there. For example, it can be required that all FTP users are in the /ftp/UserName and can not go to "/" or "/documents", for example.

To do this, we will configure the system as follows:

- We add the option "-a" in the /etc/inetd.conf file

    ## ftpacces enable (-a)
    ftp stream tcp6 nowait root /usr/lbin/ftpd ftpd -l -a

- We create the ftpaccess file with this permissions and owners:

    [noname00] root:/root # ll /etc/ftpd/ftpaccess
    -rw------- 1 bin bin 557 17 Jun 14:40 /etc/ftpd/ftpaccess

- The jailed FTP user must to belong the defined group in *guestgroup*

    [noname00] root:/root # cat /etc/ftpd/ftpaccess
    # Transfer log
    log transfers guest inbound,outbound

    # FTP user groups jailed
    guestgroup grmygroup1 grmygroup2 grmygroup3

All users belonging to the groups *grmygroup1, grmygroup2* and *grmygroup3* will be considered jailed.

In the file /etc/passwd, we will configure the jailed as follows:

   user:*:701:701:FTP Jailed User:**/ftp/user/./transfers**/:/bin/sh

As the user can not view system directories beyond /ftp/user, he will need some executables to execute basic operations (cd, ls, rm, mkdir, cut, etc.).

```
[noname00] root:/ftp/user # ls -la
total 6
drwxr-xr-x  12 root      sys         1024 15 Dic  2009 .
drwxr-xr-x   7 root      root        1024  6 Ago  2012 ..
drwxr-xr-x   2 root      sys           96 22 Jun  2011 bin
drwxr-xr-x   3 root      sys           96 15 Dic  2009 dev
drwxr-xr-x   2 root      sys           96 15 Dic  2009 etc
drwxr-xr-x   5 user      grmygroup1  1024 22 Jun  2011 files
drwxrwxrwx   3 root      sys           96 15 Dic  2009 home
drwxrwxrwx   3 root      sys           96 15 Dic  2009 opt
drwxr-xr-x   2 root      sys           96 15 Dic  2009 sbin
drwxrwxrwx   2 root      sys           96 27 Jun  2011 tmp
drwxrwxrwx   4 root      sys           96 15 Dic  2009 usr
drwxrwxrwx   3 root      sys           96 15 Dic  2009 var
[noname00] root:/ftp/user #  cd usr
[noname00] root:/ftp/user/usr # ls -la
total 6
drwxrwxrwx   4 root      sys           96 15 Dic  2009 .
drwxr-xr-x  12 root      sys         1024 15 Dic  2009 ..
drwxr-xr-x   2 root      sys         1024 22 Jun  2011 bin
drwxrwxrwx   4 root      sys         1024 15 Dic  2009 lib
```

As always, comment that this configuration may vary depending on the software version and operating system used. The important thing is to have learned the concepts. I tested this configuration on an HP-UX 11.31 and HP-UX FTPServer C.2.6.1.4.0.

Secure connections

The commands telnet, rlogin, rsh, ftp and rcp, make a connection on which the packets flowing through the network are not encrypted. This means that with a program to capture packets (called sniffers), such as Wireshark, we could capture some data such as passwords and user accounts, thereby compromising the security of our system and the information that we keep in it.

To solve this problem, the technological evolution has created hardware and software encryption.

As for the software, has expanded the use of Secure Shell (SSH) to encrypt the information packets.

Secure Shell (SSH)

This software lets us connect to a remote system through an encrypted connection. The package sent, is encrypted by a public key that can only be decrypted using the private key that is stored on the remote server. This server is responsible for generating the public and private key and sends the public to the system that has to initiate the connection. This type of encryption is called asymmetric cryptography.

To be able to use *ssh* must be running the *sshd* daemon:

```
[root@noname00 /]# ps -ef |grep ssh |grep -v grep
root      3767    1  0 15:10 ?        00:00:00 /usr/sbin/sshd
user1     4118 4103  0 15:13 ?        00:00:00 /usr/bin/ssh-agent /bin/sh -c exec -l /bin/bash -c "gnome-session"
[root@noname00 /]#
```

Creation of the public and private keys

To do this, we will use the command *ssh-keygen* as follows:

```
[user1@noname00 ~]$ ssh-keygen -t rsa
Generating public/private rsa key pair.
Enter file in which to save the key (/home/user1/.ssh/id_rsa):
Created directory '/home/user1/.ssh'.
Enter passphrase (empty for no passphrase):
Enter same passphrase again:
Your identification has been saved in /home/user1/.ssh/id_rsa.
Your public key has been saved in /home/user1/.ssh/id_rsa.pub.
The key fingerprint is:
5e:47:ac:b6:2a:0b:d7:3e:84:47:7a:50:73:d6:81:2b user1@noname00
The key's randomart image is:
+--[ RSA 2048]----+
|       o..       |
|      o +..      |
|     . + .o      |
|     . E .o      |
|      =S.+ .     |
|      oo+o o     |
|     ..+o .      |
|      o....      |
|       .oo.      |
+-----------------+
[user1@noname00 ~]$
```

With the parameter *-t* we have specified the encryption algorithm with which we want to encrypt the traffic. In this case was chosen *RSA*.

Once finished the above command, we see that has been created a new directory that contains the public and private key:

```
[user1@noname00 .ssh]$ ls -la
total 12
drwx------ 2 user1 user1   36 nov 25 19:23 .
drwx------ 8 user1 user1 4096 nov 25 19:23 ..
-rw------- 1 user1 user1 1679 nov 25 19:23 id_rsa
-rw-r--r-- 1 user1 user1  399 nov 25 19:23 id_rsa.pub
[user1@noname00 .ssh]$
```

```
[user1@noname00 .ssh]$ cat id_rsa.pub
ssh-rsa
AAAAB3NzaC1yc2EAAAABIwAAAQEAx+ShlKiZf/7/b/Zkd098mfWb6KOA
SPGnJWqhUm+dISIdIy5iJ7qUGEFK/WggJPW00frfnisDv/jT+tcLLiVpKY+kr
4pe3zX13CsBlBkiKLfTuhcoEuEu3Jhl9Srgt32XcIUxHgcC2nDdN3JM//b23edn
WW/0TOA9pnV14LTSQFhK+ojYTXXXCg6tmnXry9WAMjdVm8AYxxXhH
GeotWkS+U4w8JL07yeBPt+pp9xzyIIdYuJn+sRllnzngcbR6q2siSxGbD9ec0uU
hsvmMd62xMxV6ylvpVXppQhOYtmoUIXaGb6JgX4kXcZTfPmKzJZWqJkC
w95J8QYOzzisKdSKRw== user1@noname00
[user1@noname00 .ssh]$
```

It is of vital importance for the functioning of the connection that does not change the permissions on the directory *.ssh* or the files it contains.

Establishing a relationship of trust between keys

The contents of the public key file (id_rsa.pub) we will add it within the *authorized_keys* file of the system that wants to establish a connection with ours:

```
[user2@server2 .ssh]$ cat authorized_keys
ssh-rsa
AAAAB3NzaC1yc2EAAAABIwAAAQEAx+ShlKiZf/7/b/Zkd098mfWb6KOA
SPGnJWqhUm+dISIdIy5iJ7qUGEFK/WggJPW00frfnisDv/jT+tcLLiVpKY+kr
4pe3zX13CsBlBkiKLfTuhcoEuEu3Jhl9Srgt32XcIUxHgcC2nDdN3JM//b23edn
WW/0TOA9pnV14LTSQFhK+ojYTXXXCg6tmnXry9WAMjdVm8AYxxXhH
GeotWkS+U4w8JL07yeBPt+pp9xzyIIdYuJn+sRllnzngcbR6q2siSxGbD9ec0uU
hsvmMd62xMxV6ylvpVXppQhOYtmoUIXaGb6JgX4kXcZTfPmKzJZWqJkC
w95J8QYOzzisKdSKRw== user1@noname00
[user2@server2 .ssh]$
```

The next step is that our system try to establish an SSH connection with the system that will can connect to ours, in order to save information of this system in the file known_hosts, ending, well, the relationship of trust. The syntax of the command is:

```
[user1@noname00 .ssh]$ ssh user2@server2
The authenticity of host 'localhost (192.168.1.15)' can't be established.
RSA key fingerprint is 85:3b:c6:a0:e3:64:47:09:b6:14:86:0d:a0:52:20:d4.
```

Are you sure you want to continue connecting (yes/no)? yes
Warning: Permanently added 'localhost' (RSA) to the list of known hosts.
root@localhost's password:

[user1@noname00 .ssh]$

At the point where we asked the password for the remote user, we can cancel the process with the key combination Control-C, because we have already obtained the information we needed:

[user1@noname00 .ssh]$ cat known_hosts
server2   ssh-rsa AAAAB3NzaC1yc2EAAAABIwAAAQEA543MXZ0YESUtWrAvRn4cRDOkaN+VQceh7ycr7XMazjRpv+yFjrC83V1Q7Wq19fBj1aumlCecuy7ZdYg2mbmqMASdNWyS+eNYzeNdW/TEZuzxBcZfeEefXUfO3FJIHZcDHxwzJwpQpDprdeHS9lgn2uEDjXGQWh2tE2QvQ0Gaa94loYJStGj0dvA3gWTIBqF3jqvLq9g/285gK1ZZK91bfQQjSG2wANgJEnn/MEYl4dWB/zZxC5goHAs4tRFdscYlMK23ZZobE0jgXzzhHkk8lYeFguKuqqVfj1c71IiREnppLCYQ4fcuAcZNZnWDpp45zwcbzYvLRgcEttoXlZfJWw==
[user1@noname00 .ssh]$

From this moment on, the user *user2* of the server *server2*, can connect, by *SSH*, to the *user1* account of our system without requesting the password. Of course, traffic between the two servers will be encrypted.

Establishing a relationship of trust based on user-host relationship

In the file *$HOME/.shosts* we will add the servers and remote users who can connect to our account:

[user1@noname00 ~]$ cat .shosts
Hostname   Remote user

server2   user2
[user1@noname00 ~]$

To allow this type of authentication in the file */etc/opt/ssh/ssh_config* we will add the directives:

>   HostbasedAuthentication yes
>   EnableSSHKeysign=yes

and in */etc/opt/ssh/sshd_config* these other:

>   HostbasedAuthentication yes
>   IgnoreRhosts no

Copy a local file to a remote server

With the software package SSH comes another utility called scp that serves to copy files and directories on a remote server through an encrypted connection. The command is used as follows:

>   When copying files: scp -p file_name user@remote_server:PATH
>   When copying directories: scp -pr file_name user@remote_server:PATH

>   [user1@noname00 ~]$ scp -p vgdisplay.txt server2:$PWD
>   vgdisplay.txt   100%   16KB
>   16.4KB/s   00:00
>   [user1@noname00 ~]$

Export an environment variable remotely

The usage of *SSH* is as follows:

>   ssh remote_host -n "export VARIABLE=VALUE;
>   Command_to_execute_in_the_remote_server"

>   Example:

>   ssh noname00 –n "export PATH=$PATH:/usr/contrib/bin; my_script.sh"

Redirection of local ports

This kind of redirection is used to access remote services on the local server. The use of SSH is as follows:

> ssh [-L port:host:hostport] hostname | user@hostname
>
> **port:** It is the local port that we use to access the service.
> **host:** Machine that offers the service
> **hostport:** Port where the *host* server provides the service.
> **hostname:** Remote system to which we connect.

Example:

> [user1@noname00 ~]$ ssh -L 6464:proxy.domain.com:8080 \
>   user1@server.domain.com
> [user1@noname00 ~]$
>
> In our local server (noname00) we are using, via the local port 6464, the proxy which is running on the remote server *proxy.domain.com* through the port 8080. Then, if we configure our browser with the proxy localhost:6464, really, we are accessing to proxy.domain.com:8080.

Redirection of remote ports

It is the inverse redirect explained in the previous item. It is used to make accessible, remotely, a local port. The syntax of SSH is the following:

> ssh [-R port:host:hostport] hostname | user@hostname
>
> **port:** It is the port where it will offer the service.
> **host:** System where the service is offered.
> **hostport:** Port in which host offers the service.
> **hostname:** Remote system to which we connect.

Example:

```
ssh -fN -R 8000:localhost:8001 user1@server.domain.com
```

The service is being used in port 8000 of the local machine, will be available on port 8001 of the remote system.

Secure FTP (SFTP)

This protocol is similar to FTP, only that the file transfer is done via an encrypted connection.

Sample usage:

```
[user1@noname00 ~]$ sftp user1@server.domain.es
sftp> get file
```

Once we entered the shell of STP, we can execute the instruction *help* to get the various commands we can use:

```
sftp> help
Available commands:
    cd path                         Change remote directory to 'path'
    lcd path                        Change local directory to 'path'
    chgrp grp path                  Change group of file 'path' to
                                    'grp'
    chmod mode path                 Change permissions of file 'path'
                                    to 'mode'
    chown own path                  Change owner of file 'path' to
                                    'own'
    df [path]                       Display statistics for current
                                    directory or filesystem
                                    containing 'path'
    help                            Display this help text
    get remote-path [local-path]    Download file
    lls [ls-options [path]]         Display local directory listing
    ln oldpath newpath              Symlink remote file
    lmkdir path                     Create local directory
    lpwd                            Print local working directory
```

ls [path]	Display remote directory listing
lumask umask	Set local umask to 'umask'
mkdir path	Create remote directory
progress	Toggle display of progress meter
put local-path [remote-path]	Upload file
pwd	Display remote working directory
exit	Quit sftp
quit	Quit sftp
rename oldpath newpath	Rename remote file
rmdir path	Remove remote directory
rm path	Delete remote file
symlink oldpath newpath	Symlink remote file
version	Show SFTP version
!command	Execute 'command' in local shell
!	Escape to local shell
?	Synonym for help

sftp>

As we see, there are many commands that match those of FTP. But, SFTP is a new protocol completely independent of FTP.

Automating a SFTP connection

When we execute the same task many times, can be required to automate it. With SFTP we can save a file with the commands that we manually type and pass this file as a parameter. With an example will be clearer:

- We create a file with the following contents:

    ```
    [user1@noname00 ~]$ cat sftp.batch
    cd /
    ls
    quit
    [user1@noname00 ~]$
    ```

- We execute SFTP with the orders of the file:

```
[user1@noname00 ~]$  sftp -b sftp.batch user2@server2
Connecting to server2...
sftp> cd /
sftp> ls
.
..
.sh_history
.ssh
bin
dev
etc
home
opt
sbin
tmp
usr
var
sftp> quit
[user1@noname00 ~]$
```

CHROOT directories

A *CHROOT* directory is one that is regarded as the top level (root directory) for a user who connects to an account *STP*, that is, we can configure an account so that the user can not descend from a specific directory, for example, */sftp/user1*. This user, when types the command *cd /*, will go straight to the path */sftp/user1* instead of the real system's root directory (/). This feature is used as a protection system, because the user can not download or upload files in directories we do not want. Only will may operate below */sftp/user1*.

Then we explain the procedure for setting up a *CHROOT* directory, under a system HP-UX, but this procedure may vary depending on different versions of SSH (this is only an example to understand the concept):

- We create a new account system
- We execute the script /opt/ssh/utils/ssh_chroot_setup.sh
- We edit the file /opt/ssh/etc/sshd_config adding the following lines at the end:

Match User sftpusr
ChrootDirectory /sftp/sftpusr1

> The chroot directory must belong entirely to the root and with permissions 755, except the subdirectory home:

```
[root@noname00 ~]# cd /sftp
[root@noname00 ~]# ll
total 2
drwxr-xr-x  10 root     sys       1024  9 Sep 16:35 sftpusr1
[root@noname00 ~]# cd sftpusr1/
[root@noname00 ~]# ls -la
total 2
drwxr-xr-x  10 root     sys       1024  9 Sep 16:35 .
drwxr-xr-x   3 root     sys         96  9 Sep 15:21 ..
drwxr-xr-x   2 root     sys         96  9 Sep 15:24 bin
drwxr-xr-x   2 root     sys         96  9 Sep 16:35 dev
drwxr-xr-x   2 root     sys         96  9 Sep 15:23 etc
drwxrwxrwx   3 root     sys         96  9 Sep 16:35 home
drwxrwxrwx   3 root     sys         96  9 Sep 15:23 opt
drwxr-xr-x   2 root     sys         96  9 Sep 15:23 sbin
drwxrwxrwx   4 root     sys         96  9 Sep 15:23 usr
drwxrwxrwx   3 root     sys         96  9 Sep 15:23 var
[root@noname00 ~]#
```

> We configure the file /etc/passwd:

```
[root@noname00 ~]# grep sftpusr1 /etc/passwd
sftpusr1:*:110:20:chrooted user:/sftp/sftpusr1:/bin/sh
[root@noname00 ~]#
```

Secure Sockets Layer (SSL)

Concepts

It is a protocol for encrypting connections widely used in Web environments. Normally it is the server who has to authenticate instead of the client. This is useful to enable the user to have the assurance that is using the desired service and not a forgery. A forgery of a Web page is called Phishing and there have been instances in which it has used this method for stealing information, simulating the Web from a bank requesting personal data from our bank account, as the secret number.

When we connect to a Web page through a secure connection, we are using the HTTPS protocol, as we can see in the image below.

This protocol uses an encryption system based on SSL, which prevents the capture of packet through sniffers and provides a degree of security to the data flowing through the network.

Once established the encrypted connection, since our browser we can view the information about the digital certificate is installed on the server WEB. We will do this by double-clicking above the lock, when the page is loaded.

Also we will can do it from the menu of our browser. For example, in Firefox we will go to Edit → Preferences → View certificates.

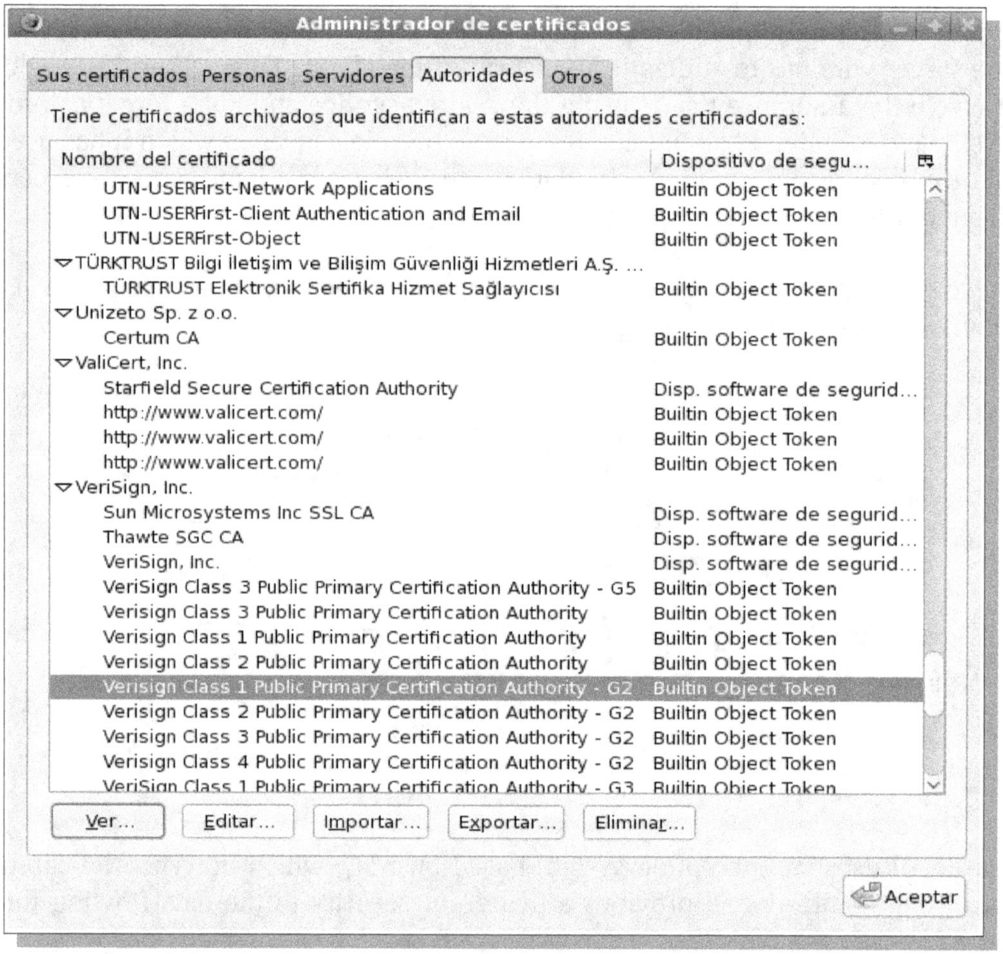

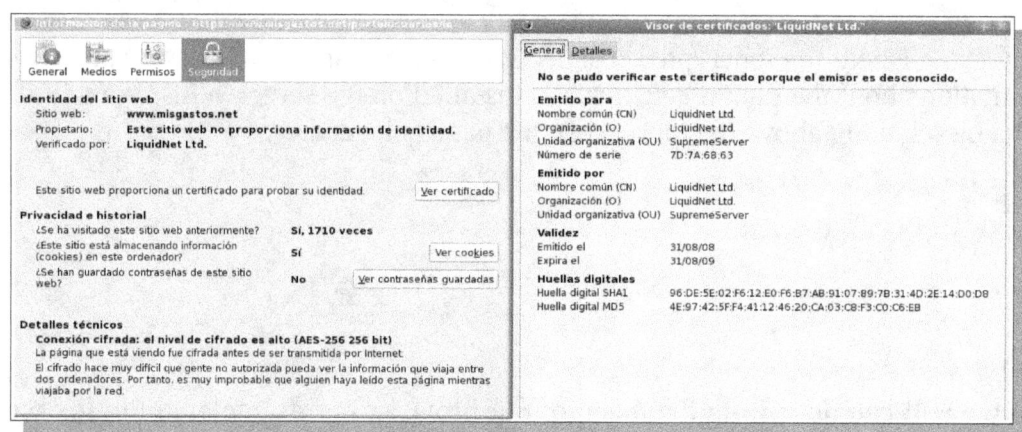

This serve to ensure us that we are connecting to the correct Web site.

There are authenticators entities recognized of digital signatures or certificates, which are responsible for issuing a certificate for Web pages, after having verified the authenticity of the company and its Web site. One of the most popular entities who are dedicated in this activity is VeriSign.

Generating a digital certificate

With the software OpenSSL, we will generate the public and the private keys, and the local certificate, to send it to the authenticator entity for they return it to us signed, and we can install it on the Web server.

Creating the file that openssl will use to generate the certificate with the relevant information

We will use the file *openssl.cnf* as described below:

```
[noname00] root:/root/scripts/certificates#cat openssl.cnf
[ req ]
default_bits        = 1024
default_keyfile     = privkey.pem
distinguished_name  = req_distinguished_name
attributes          = req_attributes
x509_extensions     = v3_ca

dirstring_type = nobmp

[ req_distinguished_name ]
countryName                = Country
countryName_default          = ES
countryName_min              = 2
countryName_max              = 2
localityName               = City
localityName_default         = Barcelona
```

```
stateOrProvinceName        = Province
stateOrProvinceName_default   = Barcelona


organizationName           = Organization Name
organizationName_default      = My_company
organizationalUnitName     = Organizational Unit Name
organizationalUnitName_default = My_company
commonName                 = Common Name (URL)
commonName_default            = www.my_company.es
commonName_max                = 64

emailAddress               = user@mail.com
emailAddress_default          = user@my_company.es
emailAddress_max              = 40


[ req_attributes ]
;challengePassword         = A challenge password
;challengePassword_min        = 4
;challengePassword_max        = 20

[ v3_ca ]

subjectKeyIdentifier=hash
authorityKeyIdentifier=keyid:always,issuer:always
basicConstraints = CA:true

[noname00] root:/root/scripts/certificates#
```

Creating the file with the public key

The script *create_key.sh* will be responsible for creating the file containing the public key:

```
[noname00] root:/root/scripts/certificates# cat create_key.sh
```

```
OPENSSL_PATH=/opt/hpws/apache/bin
export PATH=$OPENSSL_PATH:$PATH

# We create this file with a random conent
export RANDFILE=random.txt

KEY_FILE=my_key.key

# Creating the key
openssl genrsa -des3 -out $KEY_FILE 1024

# Key without encryption
openssl rsa -in $KEY_FILE -out ${KEY_FILE}.unsecure

[noname00] root:/root/scripts/certificates#
```

The file *random.txt* contains random characters.

Execution of the script:

```
[noname00] root:/root/scripts/certificates# sh create_key.sh
Generating RSA private key, 1024 bit long modulus
.....++++++
........................++++++
e is 65537 (0x10001)
Enter pass phrase for mi_clave.key:
Verifying - Enter pass phrase for mi_clave.key:
Enter pass phrase for mi_clave.key:
writing RSA key
[user1@noname00 certificates]$

[user1@noname00 certificates]$ ls -la *.key
-rw-rw-r-- 1 root root 963 nov 26 20:55 mi_clave.key
[noname00] root:/root/scripts/certificados#
```

Creating the "local" certificate

create_csr.sh will create the file with the private key:

```
[noname00] root:/root/scripts/certificates# cat create_csr.sh

OPENSSL_PATH=/opt/hpws/apache/bin
export PATH=$OPENSSL_PATH:$PATH


export OPENSSL_CONF=openssl.cnf

KEY_FILE=mi_clave.key.unsecure
CSR_FILE=mi_certificate.csr

# We create the CSR file (Certificate Signing Request)
openssl req -new -key $KEY_FILE -out $CSR_FILE

# Show CSR details
openssl req -noout -text -in  $CSR_FILE
[noname00] root:/root/scripts/certificates#
```

Execution of the script:

```
[noname00] root:/root/scripts/certificates# sh create_csr.sh
You are about to be asked to enter information that will be incorporated
into your certificate request.
What you are about to enter is what is called a Distinguished Name or a DN.
There are quite a few fields but you can leave some blank
For some fields there will be a default value,
If you enter '.', the field will be left blank.
-----
Country [ES]:
City [Barcelona]:
State [Barcelona]:
Organization Name [My_company]:
Organizational Unit Name [My_company]:
Common Name (URL) [www.my_company.es]:
address@mail.com [user@my_company.es]:

Please enter the following 'extra' attributes
to be sent with your certificate request
Certificate Request:
    Data:
```

        Version: 0 (0x0)
            Subject: C=ES, L=Barcelona, ST=Barcelona, O=My_company, OU=My_company, CN=www.my_company.es/emailAddress=user@my_company.es
        Subject Public Key Info:
            Public Key Algorithm: rsaEncryption
            RSA Public Key: (1024 bit)
                Modulus (1024 bit):
                    00:b1:a0:18:d8:87:49:4c:a9:28:77:b1:b3:86:76:
                    f0:b3:dc:68:94:9c:05:24:93:8e:ba:f5:12:bb:f5:
                    1f:4f:be:86:ed:bf:c4:c6:87:f9:f4:e8:88:65:16:
                    24:75:5f:5a:b0:73:e5:c8:dc:56:7f:70:65:1d:e4:
                    1f:f1:24:d7:d6:c1:f9:cb:cf:82:98:3a:10:be:a1:
                    9f:ba:22:d4:bd:c9:15:b8:48:17:59:1f:93:31:ec:
                    9c:19:34:df:e1:9f:c2:9d:08:e4:13:9c:57:64:6a:
                    c7:49:76:84:1d:a3:8c:5d:16:d2:4a:b1:72:69:e9:
                    8a:3c:be:10:aa:d3:c5:d7:7b
                Exponent: 65537 (0x10001)
        Attributes:
            a0:00
    Signature Algorithm: sha1WithRSAEncryption
        4c:bc:0b:ae:da:23:31:1b:19:42:06:15:ef:bb:6b:29:cf:ca:
        24:4b:c0:f6:b2:83:91:11:2f:fa:73:ea:31:e4:04:1b:f6:e7:
        80:10:74:9f:1b:64:e2:72:86:17:64:ba:53:80:7b:b8:53:c3:
        1d:a3:4d:54:5e:3c:13:08:ba:80:56:19:2a:3d:24:3e:8c:e3:
        17:de:41:c3:25:7a:27:c5:6d:ff:d1:df:e9:9a:63:d4:47:0e:
        51:6b:9b:ef:48:cf:b0:8c:fb:73:22:5e:95:fb:51:25:af:43:
        7c:8e:a8:de:1b:39:2b:9d:31:b5:d9:89:07:e4:66:da:d6:c1:
        19:94
[noname00] root:/root/scripts/certificates#

[noname00] root:/root/scripts/certificates# ls -la *.csr
-rw-rw-r-- 1 user1 user1 729 nov 26 20:57 my_certificate.csr
[noname00] root:/root/scripts/certificates#

We send the CSR the file to the authenticator entity and they will return it with another file extension: crt (my_certificate.crt). This is the signed file by the entity and is to be published on the Internet Webserver.

Sign our own certificate

If we do not want the certificate is verified by an official entity, we will can sign it ourselves but will not be a trusted certificate on the Internet. However, the user can accept its use. These certificates are used generally for services located on the Intranet (in our private local area network).

The script we used is as follows:

```
[noname00] root:/root/scripts/certificates# cat create_crt.sh

OPENSSL_PATH=/opt/hpws/apache/bin
export PATH=$OPENSSL_PATH:$PATH


export OPENSSL_CONF=openssl.cnf

CERT_FILE=my_certificate.crt
KEY_FILE=my_key.key.unsecure

openssl req -new -x509 -days 3650 -key $KEY_FILE -out $CERT_FILE

[noname00] root:/root/scripts/certificates#
```

Execution of the script:

```
[noname00] root:/root/scripts/certificates#  sh create_crt.sh
You are about to be asked to enter information that will be incorporated
into your certificate request.
What you are about to enter is what is called a Distinguished Name or a DN.
There are quite a few fields but you can leave some blank
For some fields there will be a default value,
If you enter '.', the field will be left blank.
-----
Country [ES]:
City [Barcelona]:
State [Barcelona]:
Organization Name [My_company]:
```

```
Organizational Unit Name [My_company]:
Common Name (URL) [www.my_company.es]:
address@mail.com [user@my_company.es]:
[noname00] root:/root/scripts/certificates#


[noname00] root:/root/scripts/certificates#  ls -la *.crt
-rw-rw-r-- 1 root root 1375 nov 26 20:59 my_company.crt
[noname00] root:/root/scripts/certificates#
```

Check the certificate

Once got the file CRT, we can verify that the information it contains is correct:

```
[noname00] root:/root/scripts/certificates# cat crt_test.sh

OPENSSL_PATH=/opt/hpws/apache/bin
export PATH=$OPENSSL_PATH:$PATH

CERT_FILE=my_certificate.crt
KEY_FILE=my_key.key.unsecure

# Certificate information
openssl x509 -text -in $CERT_FILE

# Check that the certificate and key make pair
openssl x509 -noout -modulus -in $CERT_FILE | openssl md5
openssl rsa -noout -modulus -in $KEY_FILE |openssl md5
[noname00] root:/root/scripts/certificates#
```

Execution of the script:

```
[noname00] root:/root/scripts/certificates# sh crt_test.sh
Certificate:
   Data:
      Version: 3 (0x2)
      Serial Number:
         dd:7e:bf:fb:80:cd:11:f2
```

Signature Algorithm: sha1WithRSAEncryption
        Issuer: C=ES, L=Barcelona, ST=Barcelona, O=My_company, OU=My_company, CN=www.my_company.es/emailAddress=user@my_company.es
    Validity
        Not Before: Nov 26 19:59:10 2008 GMT
        Not After : Nov 24 19:59:10 2018 GMT
        Subject: C=ES, L=Barcelona, ST=Barcelona, O=My_company, OU=My_company, CN=www.my_company.es/emailAddress=user@my_company.es
    Subject Public Key Info:
        Public Key Algorithm: rsaEncryption
        RSA Public Key: (1024 bit)
            Modulus (1024 bit):
                00:b1:a0:18:d8:87:49:4c:a9:28:77:b1:b3:86:76:
                f0:b3:dc:68:94:9c:05:24:93:8e:ba:f5:12:bb:f5:
                1f:4f:be:86:ed:bf:c4:c6:87:f9:f4:e8:88:65:16:
                24:75:5f:5a:b0:73:e5:c8:dc:56:7f:70:65:1d:e4:
                1f:f1:24:d7:d6:c1:f9:cb:cf:82:98:3a:10:be:a1:
                9f:ba:22:d4:bd:c9:15:b8:48:17:59:1f:93:31:ec:
                9c:19:34:df:e1:9f:c2:9d:08:e4:13:9c:57:64:6a:
                c7:49:76:84:1d:a3:8c:5d:16:d2:4a:b1:72:69:e9:
                8a:3c:be:10:aa:d3:c5:d7:7b
            Exponent: 65537 (0x10001)
    X509v3 extensions:
        X509v3 Subject Key Identifier:
            E0:57:37:77:9E:AA:04:A7:FA:07:5D:FC:82:69:7D:87:29:24:3C:CD
        X509v3 Authority Key Identifier:
            keyid:E0:57:37:77:9E:AA:04:A7:FA:07:5D:FC:82:69:7D:87:29:24:3C:CD
            DirName:/C=ES/L=Barcelona/ST=Barcelona/O=My_company/OU=My_company/CN=www.my_company.es/emailAddress=user@mycompany.es
            serial:DD:7E:BF:FB:80:CD:11:F2

        X509v3 Basic Constraints:
            CA:TRUE
    Signature Algorithm: sha1WithRSAEncryption
        07:6c:b8:2e:88:70:d3:1c:91:ad:1d:3c:7a:b6:2d:11:61:cf:
        fc:8a:14:6b:f0:2b:0c:f9:5f:da:fd:2d:86:70:6d:3e:c6:d4:
        17:02:13:be:ee:c9:a2:f1:c8:a6:de:df:07:99:84:4c:87:d8:

dd:e5:6c:88:76:36:a7:e1:7e:f8:e9:aa:21:60:9e:8c:e0:d9:
7c:97:b5:cb:c1:b4:29:49:51:0b:ec:bf:d4:8e:32:76:18:45:
bb:6a:c7:2e:33:bc:85:08:94:31:2a:ba:e1:bd:95:a0:81:97:
40:4b:37:b4:1e:32:f4:3f:ce:d7:98:a4:20:a8:74:7b:f5:f3:
b7:df

-----BEGIN CERTIFICATE-----
MIIDyzCCAzSgAwIBAgIJAN1+v/uAzRHyMA0GCSqGSIb3DQEBBQUAMI
GgMQswCQYD
VQQGEwJFUzESMBAGA1UEBxMJQmFyY2Vsb25hMRIwEAYDVQQIEwl
CYXJjZWxvbmEx
EzARBgNVBAoUCk1pX2VtcHJlc2ExEzARBgNVBAsUCk1pX2VtcHJlc2Ex
GTAXBgNV
BAMTEHd3dy5taWVtcHJlc2EuZXMxJDAiBgkqhkiG9w0BCQEWFWNvbnR
hY3RvQG1p
ZW1wcmVzYS5lczAeFw0wODExMjYxOTU5MTBaFw0xODExMjQxOTU5
MTBaMIGgMQsw
CQYDVQQGEwJFUzESMBAGA1UEBxMJQmFyY2Vsb25hMRIwEAYDVQ
QIEwlCYXJjZWxvbmEx
bmExEzARBgNVBAoUCk1pX2VtcHJlc2ExEzARBgNVBAsUCk1pX2VtcHJlc2Ex
c2ExGTAX
BgNVBAMTEHd3dy5taWVtcHJlc2EuZXMxJDAiBgkqhkiG9w0BCQEWFW
NvbnRhY3Rv
QG1pZW1wcmVzYS5lczCBnzANBgkqhkiG9w0BAQEFAAOBjQAwgYkCgY
EAsaAY2IdJ
TKkod7Gzhnbws9xolJwFJJOOuvUSu/UfT76G7b/Exof59OiIZRYkdV9asHPly
NxW
f3BlHeQf8STX1sH5y8+CmDoQvqGfuiLUvckVuEgXWR+TMeycGTTf4Z/Cn
QjkE5xX
ZGrHSXaEHaOMXRbSSrFyaemKPL4QqtPF13sCAwEAAaOCAQkwggEFM
B0GA1UdDgQW
BBTgVzd3nqoEp/oHXfyCaX2HKSQ8zTCB1QYDVR0jBIHNMIHKgBTgVzd
3nqoEp/oH
XfyCaX2HKSQ8zaGBpqSBozCBoDELMAkGA1UEBhMCRVMxEjAQBgNV
BAcTCUJhcmNl
bG9uYTESMBAGA1UECBMJQmFyY2Vsb25hMRMwEQYDVQQKFApNaV
9lbXByZXNhMRMw
EQYDVQQLFApNaV9lbXByZXNhMRkwFwYDVQQDExB3d3cubWllbXBy
ZXNhLmVzMSQw
IgYJKoZIhvcNAQkBFhVjb250YWN0b0BtaWVtcHJlc2EuZXOCCQDdfr/7gM
0R8jAM

BgNVHRMEBTADAQH/MA0GCSqGSIb3DQEBBQUAA4GBAAdsuC6IcN
Mcka0dPHq2LRFh
z/yKFGvwKwz5X9r9LYZwbT7G1BcCE77uyaLxyKbe3weZhEyH2N3lbIh2Nq
fhfvjp
qiFgnozg2XyXtcvBtClJUQvsv9SOMnYYRbtqxy4zvIUIlDEquuG9laCBl0BLN
7Qe
MvQ/zteYpCCodHv187ff
-----END CERTIFICATE-----
76bb7dfc4a0d281beb6914024eed83d9
76bb7dfc4a0d281beb6914024eed83d9
[noname00] root:/root/scripts/certificates#

Configuring the Webserver to use the certificate generated

After completing all the steps above, it has to configure the Webserver to use the digital certificate. Each Webmaster will know how to do it according to the Web server he is using. For example, in the Apache Webserver, and without wanting to deepen as it is set a web server, we will edit the file ssl.conf adding the following lines in the VirtualHost section which is need:

SSLCertificateFile /root/scripts/certificates/my_certificate.crt
SSLCertificateKeyFile /root/scripts/certificates/my_key.key.unsecure

The mail server *sendmail*

Concepts

The email was invented by Ray Tomlinson in 1971. Today, *Sendmail* is the mail server used for excellence in UNIX systems. Its configuration can be costly even for a systems administrator experienced due to the high flexibility offered by this product. The best way to see all corners of configuration is to visit the official website of the supplier: http://www.sendmail.org, however, in this chapter we will try to create a simple mail server.

The configuration file is usually in */etc/mail/sendmail.cf*. We can use a program *M4* macro processor that runs the functions defined in the file *sendmail.mc* for, well, create the file *sendmail.cf* definitive.

Apart from the two files previously commented, *sendmail* can also use the following:

- **local-host-names:** It indicates what domains belong the mail server.
- **access:** It contains the IPs that can use the mail server.
- **mailertable:** Routing for domains, this is, a mail addressed to *my_company.com* can be redirected to *smtp.my_company.com*.
- **alias:** Allows us to redirect the mail to a recipient list or add an alias for a user. Example:

    # Project developers
    project: diego@mycompany.com,silvia@mycompany.com,david@mycompany.com

    Once we have configured this file, we must to rebuild the database that uses sendmail with the command */usr/bin/newaliases*.

Configuring a mail server

- In the file *local-hosts-names* we indicate that our server will belong to the domain *my_company.com*.

  [root@noname00 mail]# cat local-host-names
  # local-host-names - include all aliases for your machine here.
  localhost
  my_company.com
  [root@noname00 mail]#

- In the file *access*, we enable IPs or networks of trust to be able to use the mail server:

  [root@noname00 mail]# cat access
  # Check the /usr/share/doc/sendmail/README.cf file for a description
  # of the format of this file. (search for access_db in that file)
  # The /usr/share/doc/sendmail/README.cf is part of the sendmail-doc
  # package.
  #
  # If you want to use AuthInfo with "M:PLAIN LOGIN", make sure to have the
  # cyrus-sasl-plain package installed.
  #
  # By default we allow relaying from localhost...
  Connect:localhost   RELAY
  Connect:192.168.1   RELAY
  [root@noname00 mail]#

- We configure the file macros *sendmail.mc*:

  The lines that have been modified with respect to the original file are as follows:

  [root@noname00 mail]# cat sendmail.mc
  divert(-1)dnl
  dnl #
  dnl # This is the sendmail macro config file for m4. If you make changes to
  dnl # /etc/mail/sendmail.mc, you will need to regenerate the
  dnl # /etc/mail/sendmail.cf file by confirming that the sendmail-cf package is

dnl # installed and then performing a
dnl #
dnl #   make -C /etc/mail
dnl #
VERSIONID(`setup for linux')dnl
OSTYPE(`linux')dnl

dnl
# noname00 is our intelligent host (smart host), using "uucp-new".
define(`SMART_HOST', `uucp-new:noname00')
dnl
# Allow use of transport protocols local mail, smtp y uucp.
MAILER(`local')
MAILER(`smtp')
MAILER(`uucp')
LOCAL_NET_CONFIG
This rule ensures that all local mail is delivered using SMTP transport, everything else will go for the smart host.
R$* < @ $* .$m. > $* $#smtp $@ $2.$m. $: $1 < @ $2.$m. > $3
dnl
fin
[root@noname00 mail]#

The complete file would be as follows:

[root@noname00 mail]# cat sendmail.mc
divert(-1)dnl
dnl #
dnl # This is the sendmail macro config file for m4. If you make changes to
dnl # /etc/mail/sendmail.mc, you will need to regenerate the
dnl # /etc/mail/sendmail.cf file by confirming that the sendmail-cf package is
dnl # installed and then performing a
dnl #
dnl #   make -C /etc/mail
dnl #
include(`/usr/share/sendmail-cf/m4/cf.m4')dnl
VERSIONID(`setup for linux')dnl
OSTYPE(`linux')dnl

```
dnl #
dnl # Do not advertize sendmail version.
dnl #
dnl define(`confSMTP_LOGIN_MSG', `$j Sendmail; $b')dnl
dnl #
dnl # default logging level is 9, you might want to set it higher to
dnl # debug the configuration
dnl #
dnl define(`confLOG_LEVEL', `9')dnl
dnl #
dnl # Uncomment and edit the following line if your outgoing mail needs to
dnl # be sent out through an external mail server:
dnl #
dnl define(`SMART_HOST', `smtp.your.provider')dnl
dnl #
define(`confDEF_USER_ID',``8:12'')dnl
dnl define(`confAUTO_REBUILD')dnl
define(`confTO_CONNECT', `1m')dnl
define(`confTRY_NULL_MX_LIST', `True')dnl
define(`confDONT_PROBE_INTERFACES', `True')dnl
define(`PROCMAIL_MAILER_PATH', `/usr/bin/procmail')dnl
define(`ALIAS_FILE', `/etc/aliases')dnl
define(`STATUS_FILE', `/var/log/mail/statistics')dnl
define(`UUCP_MAILER_MAX', `2000000')dnl
define(`confUSERDB_SPEC', `/etc/mail/userdb.db')dnl
define(`confPRIVACY_FLAGS', `authwarnings,novrfy,noexpn,restrictqrun')dnl
define(`confAUTH_OPTIONS', `A')dnl
dnl #
dnl # The following allows relaying if the user authenticates, and disallows
dnl # plaintext authentication (PLAIN/LOGIN) on non-TLS links
dnl #
dnl define(`confAUTH_OPTIONS', `A p')dnl
dnl #
dnl # PLAIN is the preferred plaintext authentication method and used by
dnl # Mozilla Mail and Evolution, though Outlook Express and other MUAs do
dnl # use LOGIN. Other mechanisms should be used if the connection is not
dnl # guaranteed secure.
dnl # Please remember that saslauthd needs to be running for AUTH.
dnl #
dnl TRUST_AUTH_MECH(`EXTERNAL  DIGEST-MD5  CRAM-MD5
```

LOGIN PLAIN')dnl
dnl define(`confAUTH_MECHANISMS', `EXTERNAL GSSAPI DIGEST-MD5 CRAM-MD5 LOGIN PLAIN')dnl
dnl #
dnl # Rudimentary information on creating certificates for sendmail TLS:
dnl #   cd /etc/pki/tls/certs; make sendmail.pem
dnl # Complete usage:
dnl #   make -C /etc/pki/tls/certs usage
dnl #
dnl define(`confCACERT_PATH', `/etc/pki/tls/certs')dnl
dnl define(`confCACERT', `/etc/pki/tls/certs/ca-bundle.crt')dnl
dnl define(`confSERVER_CERT', `/etc/pki/tls/certs/sendmail.pem')dnl
dnl define(`confSERVER_KEY', `/etc/pki/tls/certs/sendmail.pem')dnl
dnl #
dnl # This allows sendmail to use a keyfile that is shared with OpenLDAP's
dnl # slapd, which requires the file to be readble by group ldap
dnl #
dnl define(`confDONT_BLAME_SENDMAIL', `groupreadablekeyfile')dnl
dnl #
dnl define(`confTO_QUEUEWARN', `4h')dnl
dnl define(`confTO_QUEUERETURN', `5d')dnl
dnl define(`confQUEUE_LA', `12')dnl
dnl define(`confREFUSE_LA', `18')dnl
define(`confTO_IDENT', `0')dnl
dnl FEATURE(delay_checks)dnl
FEATURE(`no_default_msa', `dnl')dnl
FEATURE(`smrsh', `/usr/sbin/smrsh')dnl
FEATURE(`mailertable', `hash -o /etc/mail/mailertable.db')dnl
FEATURE(`virtusertable', `hash -o /etc/mail/virtusertable.db')dnl
FEATURE(redirect)dnl
FEATURE(always_add_domain)dnl
FEATURE(use_cw_file)dnl
FEATURE(use_ct_file)dnl
dnl #
dnl # The following limits the number of processes sendmail can fork to accept
dnl # incoming messages or process its message queues to 20.) sendmail refuses
dnl # to accept connections once it has reached its quota of child processes.
dnl #
dnl define(`confMAX_DAEMON_CHILDREN', `20')dnl
dnl #

dnl # Limits the number of new connections per second. This caps the overhead
dnl # incurred due to forking new sendmail processes. May be useful against
dnl # DoS attacks or barrages of spam. (As mentioned below, a per-IP address
dnl # limit would be useful but is not available as an option at this writing.)
dnl #
dnl define(`confCONNECTION_RATE_THROTTLE', `3')dnl
dnl #
dnl # The -t option will retry delivery if e.g. the user runs over his quota.
dnl #
FEATURE(local_procmail, `', `procmail -t -Y -a $h -d $u')dnl
FEATURE(`access_db', `hash -T<TMPF> -o /etc/mail/access.db')dnl
FEATURE(`blacklist_recipients')dnl
EXPOSED_USER(`root')dnl
dnl #
dnl # For using Cyrus-IMAPd as POP3/IMAP server through LMTP delivery uncomment
dnl # the following 2 definitions and activate below in the MAILER section the
dnl # cyrusv2 mailer.
dnl #
dnl define(`confLOCAL_MAILER', `cyrusv2')dnl
dnl define(`CYRUSV2_MAILER_ARGS', `FILE /var/lib/imap/socket/lmtp')dnl
dnl #
dnl # The following causes sendmail to only listen on the IPv4 loopback address
dnl # 127.0.0.1 and not on any other network devices. Remove the loopback
dnl # address restriction to accept email from the internet or intranet.
dnl #
dnl # DAEMON_OPTIONS(`Port=smtp,Addr=127.0.0.1, Name=MTA')dnl
dnl #
dnl # The following causes sendmail to additionally listen to port 587 for
dnl # mail from MUAs that authenticate. Roaming users who can't reach their
dnl # preferred sendmail daemon due to port 25 being blocked or redirected find
dnl # this useful.
dnl #
dnl DAEMON_OPTIONS(`Port=submission, Name=MSA, M=Ea')dnl
dnl #
dnl # The following causes sendmail to additionally listen to port 465, but
dnl # starting immediately in TLS mode upon connecting. Port 25 or 587 followed
dnl # by STARTTLS is preferred, but roaming clients using Outlook Express can't

dnl # do STARTTLS on ports other than 25. Mozilla Mail can ONLY use STARTTLS
dnl # and doesn't support the deprecated smtps; Evolution <1.1.1 uses smtps
dnl # when SSL is enabled-- STARTTLS support is available in version 1.1.1.
dnl #
dnl # For this to work your OpenSSL certificates must be configured.
dnl #
dnl DAEMON_OPTIONS(`Port=smtps, Name=TLSMTA, M=s')dnl
dnl #
dnl # The following causes sendmail to additionally listen on the IPv6 loopback
dnl # device. Remove the loopback address restriction listen to the network.
dnl #
dnl DAEMON_OPTIONS(`port=smtp,Addr=::1, Name=MTA-v6, Family=inet6')dnl
dnl #
dnl # enable both ipv6 and ipv4 in sendmail:
dnl #
dnl DAEMON_OPTIONS(`Name=MTA-v4, Family=inet, Name=MTA-v6, Family=inet6')
dnl #
dnl # We strongly recommend not accepting unresolvable domains if you want to
dnl # protect yourself from spam. However, the laptop and users on computers
dnl # that do not have 24x7 DNS do need this.
dnl #
FEATURE(`accept_unresolvable_domains')dnl
dnl #
dnl FEATURE(`relay_based_on_MX')dnl
dnl #
dnl # Also accept email sent to "localhost.localdomain" as local email.
dnl #
LOCAL_DOMAIN(`localhost.localdomain')dnl
dnl #
dnl # The following example makes mail from this host and any additional
dnl # specified domains appear to be sent from mydomain.com
dnl #
MASQUERADE_AS(myalias.es)dnl
dnl #
dnl # masquerade not just the headers, but the envelope as well
dnl #

```
dnl FEATURE(masquerade_envelope)dnl
dnl #
dnl # masquerade not just @mydomainalias.com, but @*.mydomainalias.com as well
dnl #
FEATURE(masquerade_entire_domain)dnl
dnl #
MASQUERADE_DOMAIN(localhost)dnl
MASQUERADE_DOMAIN(localhost.localdomain)dnl
MASQUERADE_DOMAIN(my_company.com)dnl
MAILER(smtp)dnl
MAILER(procmail)dnl
MAILER(cyrusv2)dnl
MAILER(`local')
MAILER(`uucp')
LOCAL_NET_CONFIG
# This rule ensures that all local mail is delivered using SMTP transport, everything else will go for the smart host.
R$* < @ $* .$m. > $*        $#smtp $@ $2.$m. $: $1 < @ $2.$m. > $3
dnl
#
# fin
[root@noname00 mail]#
```

- Create the *sendmail.cf* and restart the service:

```
[root@noname00 mail]# m4 /etc/mail/sendmail.mc > /etc/sendmail.cf
[root@noname00 mail]# make -C /etc/mail
make: Se entered into the directory `/etc/mail'
make: Nothing to do for `all'.
make: exits the directory `/etc/mail'
[root@noname00 mail]# /etc/init.d/sendmail stop
Deactivation de sm-client:                    [ OK ]
Propaganda down sendmail:                     [ OK ]
[root@noname00 mail]# /etc/init.d/sendmail start
Starting sendmail:                  [ OK ]
Init  sm-client:                 [ OK ]
[root@noname00 mail]#
```

We check that port 25 (SMTP) is listening after the boot:

```
[root@noname00 mail]# netstat -an |grep LISTEN  |grep 25
tcp    0    0 0.0.0.0:25           0.0.0.0:*              LISTEN
```

The sendmail.cf file is too long to be right show all its contents in this book.

Masking

The line *MASQUERADE_DOMAIN (my_company.com) dnl* of the file *sendmail.mc*, indicates we are adding an alias called my_company.*com*. This means that our emails may also be sent as *user@my_company.com*.

Message queue

A mail server is designed to be used by many users. Obviously, all the mails that are sent can not do it at once and for that reason there is a messages queue that is going processed in an orderly manner.

We will check messages waiting to send with the following command:

```
[root@noname00 mail]# sendmail -bp
/var/spool/mqueue is empty
                Total requests: 0
[root@noname00 mail]#
```

and remove erasing the contents of the directory */var/spool/mqueue*.

Relay

Can be given the case that in our local network, only one server has configured *sendmail* to send mails to the outside and the rest of the systems of the network are configured it to send their messages to this central server, which, will forward the emails to their final destination. This structure of sending mail is the called *relay*.

For a mail server can send their messages to the central server, simply put the directive *DLName_of_the_central_server* in the file *sendmail.cf* or add a line of this style *define(`SMART_HOST', `relay.DOMAIN.com)dnl* in the file *sendmail.mc*.

Time synchronization via NTP

The initials NTP correspond to Network Time Protocol and is a communications protocol used to synchronize computer clocks across the network. UDP port 123 is used to connect to time servers.

There are different levels of time servers. The level 0, correspond to the GPS clocks or atomic clocks, while the level 1 gets the time from level 0 time servers, and so on.

For a UNIX system can synchronize its clock with a time server, is necesary to have installed, configured and running the NTP software. Typically, this software is already installed with the base operating system software and we will see running the ntpd daemon.

```
[root@noname00 ~]# ps -ef |grep -i ntpd |grep -v grep
ntp       1571     1  0 19:23 ?        00:00:00 ntpd -u ntp:ntp -p /var/run/ntpd.pid -g
[root@noname00 ~]#
```

To configure the NTP client, again, depends on the version of UNIX we are using. For example, on a Linux system, as a general rule, we will configure the file /etc/ntp.conf. The most important are the lines server *NameNTPServer*, because that is where we set the time server with which we want to synchronize.

```
[root@rd00 ~]# cat /etc/ntp.conf
# For more information about this file, see the man pages
# ntp.conf(5), ntp_acc(5), ntp_auth(5), ntp_clock(5), ntp_misc(5), ntp_mon(5).

driftfile /var/lib/ntp/drift

# Permit time synchronization with our time source, but do not
# permit the source to query or modify the service on this system.
restrict default kod nomodify notrap nopeer noquery
restrict -6 default kod nomodify notrap nopeer noquery

# Permit all access over the loopback interface.  This could
```

```
# be tightened as well, but to do so would effect some of
# the administrative functions.
restrict 127.0.0.1
restrict -6 ::1

# Hosts on local network are less restricted.
#restrict 192.168.1.0 mask 255.255.255.0 nomodify notrap

# Use public servers from the pool.ntp.org project.
# Please consider joining the pool (http://www.pool.ntp.org/join.html).
server 0.fedora.pool.ntp.org iburst
server 1.fedora.pool.ntp.org iburst
server 2.fedora.pool.ntp.org iburst
server 3.fedora.pool.ntp.org iburst

#broadcast 192.168.1.255 autokey      # broadcast server
#broadcastclient                       # broadcast client
#broadcast 224.0.1.1 autokey           # multicast server
#multicastclient 224.0.1.1             # multicast client
#manycastserver 239.255.254.254        # manycast server
#manycastclient 239.255.254.254 autokey # manycast client

# Undisciplined Local Clock. This is a fake driver intended for backup
# and when no outside source of synchronized time is available.
#server   127.127.1.0        # local clock
#fudge    127.127.1.0 stratum 10

# Enable public key cryptography.
#crypto

includefile /etc/ntp/crypto/pw

# Key file containing the keys and key identifiers used when operating
# with symmetric key cryptography.
keys /etc/ntp/keys

# Specify the key identifiers which are trusted.
#trustedkey 4 8 42

# Specify the key identifier to use with the ntpdc utility.
```

>#requestkey 8
>
>\# Specify the key identifier to use with the ntpq utility.
>#controlkey 8
>
>\# Enable writing of statistics records.
>#statistics clockstats cryptostats loopstats peerstats
>[root@rd00 ~]#

Once we have configured NTP client, we must configure our location on Earth so we can get the correct time. On a Linux system we will find the file /etc/localtime, which is usually a link to the file containing the information of our zone, for example, /usr/share/zoneinfo/Europe/Madrid.

The printing system

PostScript

In 1984, John Warnock, Check Geschke, Doug Brotz, Ed Taft and Bill Paxton, of the company Adobe, developed the printing system PostScript (PS) which finally has become a standard.

PS is an interpreted programming language capable of producing a high quality printed content, including rich text and images, independent of the output device. Represented a technological revolution in media and publishing books because, until then, were limited to the private printing. PS gave them the opportunity to make a leap in quality and a touch of personal mark.

The end user who uses the printer, probably does not even know of the existence of PS, since own text editors such as OpenOffice, are responsible for translating the document into language PS. For those printers that do not support PS, there is an interpreter called GhostScript which is responsible for submitting data PS and PDF (Portable Document Format) on screen and, also, prepare it for they can be printed on a printer with graphics capabilities through the actual driver for this hardware.

A script PostScript has a structure similar to this:

```
newpath
% Cursor initialization
100 100 moveto
% Drawing the rectangle
400 130 lineto
400 280 lineto
100 250 lineto
100 100 lineto
```

stroke

/Times-Roman findfont
15 scalefont

setfont

100 500 moveto

(Text) show

If we are interested to know more about the programming language PostScript, we can steer to the official website of Adobe http://www.adobe.com/devnet/postscript/.

Commands related to the printing system

In UNIX systems, there is a printing service or daemon which can vary according to the distribution or version of our system. The daemons of printing more used are *lpd*, *lpshed* and *cups*. Its function is to review whether there are jobs queued to be printed. These processes using the file */etc/printcap* to store the printer settings:

```
[root@noname00 ~]# cat /etc/printcap
# This file was automatically generated by cupsd(8) from the
# /etc/cups/printers.conf file.  All changes to this file
# will be lost.
Stylus-DX4800|EPSON Stylus DX4800:rm=noname00.casita.es:rp=Stylus-DX4800:
[root@noname00 ~]#
```

Following is a list of UNIX commands related to the printing system:

> **lpr:** Serves to send jobs to the print queue.

  Syntax:

   lpr [-Pimp] [-h] [-#Num] [files]

-Pimp → We specify what printer we will send the jobs.
-h → Eliminates the first page header.
-#Num → We set the number of copies in print.

[root@noname00 ~]# lpr -P Stylus-DX4800 test.txt

> **lpq:** We analyze the state of the print queue.

   -a → We see the status of all print queues.

   [root@noname00 ~]# lpq -P Stylus-DX4800
   Stylus-DX4800 is ready
   there are no entries
   [root@noname00 ~]#

> **lprm**: Cancel print jobs.

   Syntax

   lprm [-Pimp] [-] [Work #] [Usr]

> **lpc:** We check the status of all printers.

   [root@noname00 ~]# lpc status
   Stylus-DX4800:
   printer in device 'usb' speed -1
   The queue is ready
   Printing is enabled
   There are no entries
   This demon
   [root@noname00 ~]#

> **lpadmin:** Serves to configure a printer.
> **lp *file.txt*:** Prints de file *file.txt*.

   -d dest → We select the printer.
   -m → When finished printing, we will receive an email.
   -n num → Number of copies.

> **lpstat:** It gives us information on the current state of the printing system. Then

we attach an example in which we see the printing jobs of the user *user1* and we cancel it:

```
[root@noname00 ~]# lpstat -U user1
Stylus-DX4800-24        user1           97280   sáb 13 dic 2008 08:13:07 CET
[root@noname00 ~]# cancel -u user1
[root@noname00 ~]# lpstat -U user1
[root@noname00 ~]#
```

Note: cancel isa command in the CUPS printing system.

SAMBA-CIFS

SMB/CIFS is a protocol for sharing files and printers with other Windows or UNIX systems, in the same local network.

The configuration file is usually in the directory */etc/samba/smb.conf* and is structured as follows:

- **workgroup:** Sets the name of a working group. Must match in both Windows and UNIX.
- **Access permissions to servers:** In the directive *hosts allow = 192.168.1. localhots,* we are establishing the networks or IP addresses that can access shared resources.
- **Access permissions to users:** In the parameter *valid users = user1 user2, etc.* we are establishing users who have access to shared resources.
- Sharing resources: When in the configuration file will see a section of the style:

    [homes]
    comment = Home Directories
    ;browseable = yes
    writable = yes
    create mask = 0777
    directory mask = 0777
    ;valid users = %S
    ;valid users = MYDOMAIN\%S

means:

    [name of the shared resource]
    comment = My shared resource
    path = /directory_of_the_system
    browseable = yes   → The resource is visible
    writable = yes   → The resource is writable
    create mask = 0777
    directory mask = 0777

For example, we could add a section to share photos as follows:

```
[WindowsD]
comment = Photos
path = /images/vacation
browseable = yes
writeable = yes
create mask = 0777
directory mask = 0777
guest ok = yes

[CDRom]
comment = Shared CD Rom
path = /media/cdrom0
public = yes
writable = no
browseable = yes
```

Once we have finished configuring the file *smb.conf*, we will have to reboot *SAMBA* to get access to shared resources:

/etc/init.d/smb restart

In Windows we can access using the network environment.

To access the resources shared by Windows, if we use Konqueror or Nautils, it is as simple as typing in the address bar:

smb://Windows_hostname

We may also use the command line as follows:

- **smbclient -L <host>** → It shows the shared resources in the system *<host>*.
- **smbmount //host/name_of_the_resource /mnt/samba** → It will show us the share called *name_of_the_resource* in the directory */mnt/samba*. To specify the user name we use:

    smbmount //host/ name_of_the_resource /mnt/samba -o username=<user>

- **smbclient -L <host>** → It shows the shared resources in the system *<host>*.
- **nmblookup <host>** → Return the <host> present in the network.

- **nbtscan <red/mascara>** → will scan the network looking for computers that share resources. Example:

    nbtscan 192.168.0.0/24

- **smbstatus** → Allows see who is connected to the Samba server.

If we want to mount a file system SAMBA during boot, we will have to configure */etc/fstab* like this:

    //images/vacations /mnt/samba smbfs username=*user1*,user,noauto,rw 0 0

The file *smbusers* establishes a connection between the user of the system and the user client *SAMBA*:

    [root@noname00 samba]# cat smbusers
    # Unix_name = SMB_name1 SMB_name2 ...
    nobody = guest pcguest smbguest
    root = Administrator david
    David = david
    [root@noname00 samba]#

If we do not want to assign a password to the user *SAMBA* distinct to that contained in the file */etc/passwd*, we must authenticate by *SAMBA:*

    [root@noname00 samba]# smbpasswd -a David
    New SMB password:
    Retype new SMB password:
    [root@noname00 samba]#

Example of configuration:

[root@noname00 samba]# grep -v "#" smb.conf

[global]

       workgroup = SMBWRKGRP
       server string = Samba Server Version %v
;   encrypt passwords = yes
       netbios name = vmnoname00

       interfaces = lo eth0 eth1 vmnet0 vmnet1 vmnet8 192.168.165.1/24 172.16.52.1/24 192.168.78.1/24
       hosts allow = ALL

       log file = /var/log/samba/log.%m
       max log size = 50

       security = share
       passdb backend = tdbsam

;   realm = MY_REALM

;   password server = <NT-Server-Name>

;   domain master = yes
;   domain logons = yes

;   logon script = %m.bat
;   logon script = %u.bat
;   logon path = \\%L\Profiles\%u
;   logon path =

;   add user script = /usr/sbin/useradd "%u" -n -g users
;   add group script = /usr/sbin/groupadd "%g"
;   add machine script = /usr/sbin/useradd -n -c "Workstation (%u)" -M -d /nohome -s /bin/false "%u"

```
;       delete user script = /usr/sbin/userdel "%u"
;       delete user from group script = /usr/sbin/userdel "%u" "%g"
;       delete group script = /usr/sbin/groupdel "%g"


;       local master = no
;       os level = 33
;       preferred master = yes


;       wins support = yes
;       wins server = w.x.y.z
;       wins proxy = yes

;       dns proxy = yes


;       load printers = yes
        cups options = raw

;       printcap name = /etc/printcap
;       printcap name = lpstat
;       printing = cups


;       map archive = no
;       map hidden = no
;       map read only = no
;       map system = no
        username map = /etc/samba/smbusers
;       guest ok = no
;       guest account = nobody
;       store dos attributes = yes



[homes]
        comment = Home Directories
;       browseable = yes
        writable = yes
```

```
            create mask = 0777
            directory mask = 0777
;           valid users = %S
;           valid users = MYDOMAIN\%S

[WindowsD]
            comment = Shared photos
            path = /photos
;           browseable = yes
            writeable = yes
            create mask = 0777
            directory mask = 0777
            guest ok = yes


[printers]
            comment = All Printers
            path = /var/spool/samba
            browseable = yes
            guest ok = yes
;           writable = No
            printable = yes
            printer name = Epson_Stylus_DX4800
            use client driver = yes

;           [netlogon]
;           comment = Network Logon Service
;           path = /var/lib/samba/netlogon
;           guest ok = yes
;           writable = no
;           share modes = no



;           [Profiles]
;           path = /var/lib/samba/profiles
;           browseable = no
;           guest ok = yes



;           [public]
;           comment = Public Stuff
```

```
;       path = /home/samba
;       public = yes
;       writable = yes
;       printable = no
;       write list = +staff

[WindowsC]
        comment = Public directory
        path = /public
        writeable = yes
;       browseable = yes
        guest ok = yes
[root@noname00 samba]#
```

Shell script

Interprets of commands

All instructions that have been introduced throughout this book have been written through a command line, also called *shell*.

In the UNIX world there are several types of shell. Among the highlights are:

- **Bourne shell (sh):** Was developed by Stephen Borune of Bell Laboratories of AT&T. It is the first shell was created and, although it is a bit limited, the most modern shells have inherited many of its features, such as the ability to program *scripts*.

    A script is a program written in the programming language itself from the shell. It is can use variables, functions, loops, conditions and system commands.

- **C shell (csh):** Was developed by Bill Joy in the Berkeley University, California. This shell was created with the intention that its syntax was similar to that of the C programming language. Introduced new concepts such as the ability to perform arithmetic operations.

- **Bourne shell again (bash):** It is based in *Bourne shell* and is one of the most complete Shells and, therefore, extended in the UNIX world because of its strength as a programming language, besides other developments that have been implemented in each of its versions.

    Brian Fox began to develop it in 1987 but, at present, Chet Ramey is who is responsible for its development for the GNU project.

- **Korn shell (ksh):** It was developed by David Korn of Bell Laboratories of AT&T. It is also based in Bourne shell and, along with bash, is the shell more extended. Scripts made with *ksh* and *bash* have a high degree of compatibility.

When the system administrator creates a new user account, it is linked to a shell:

```
[root@noname00 ~]# grep usuer1 /etc/passwd
user1:x:601:601:My first user:/home/user1:/bin/bash
[root@noname00 ~]#
```

Each time a user authenticates into the system is running a script. In *korn shell* this file is called *.profile* and, in *bash*, *.bashrc*. This serves to run a series of instructions, to call another script or to load environment some variables automatically each time we go into the system.

Example:

```
[user1@noname00 ~]$ ls -la
total 40
drwx------ 9 user1 user1 4096 dic  1 14:35 .
drwxr-xr-x 6 root  root    61 nov  3 16:48 ..
-rw------- 1 user1 user1 2396 nov 26 21:03 .bash_history
-rw-r--r-- 1 user1 user1   18 feb 29  2008 .bash_logout
-rw-r--r-- 1 user1 user1  176 feb 29  2008 .bash_profile
-rw-r--r-- 1 user1 user1  191 dic  1 14:35 .bashrc
drwxrwxr-x 2 user1 user1 4096 nov 26 21:00 certificados
drwxrwxr-x 2 user1 user1   24 nov  8 08:10 files
drwx------ 2 user1 user1    6 nov  3 17:07 .gconf
drwx------ 2 user1 user1   24 nov  3 17:08 .gconfd
drwxr-xr-x 3 user1 user1   21 nov  3 17:07 .gnome2
drwxr-xr-x 4 user1 user1   37 may 30  2008 .mozilla
-rw------- 1 user1 user1   50 nov  8 06:46 .sh_history
-rw-rw-r-- 1 user1 user1   44 nov 25 19:50 .shosts
drwx------ 2 user1 user1   54 nov 25 19:39 .ssh
-rw------- 1 user1 user1 4590 dic  1 14:35 .viminfo
[user1@noname00 ~]$

[user1@noname00 ~]$ cat .bashrc
# .bashrc

# Source global definitions
if [ -f /etc/bashrc ]; then
        . /etc/bashrc
fi
```

User specific aliases and functions

echo I am the user user1 and I am using the shell $SHELL
[user1@noname00 ~]$

[root@noname00 ~]# su - user1
I am the user user1 and I am using the shell /bin/bash
[user1@noname00 ~]$

Ways to run a script

A script can be run in different ways. We will use the following in order to show them:

[user1@noname00 scripts]$ cat hello_world.sh
echo Hello World
[user1@noname00 scripts]$

- Using the shell that is programmed, followed by the name of the script:

    [user1@noname00 scripts]$ bash hello_world.sh
    Hello World
    [user1@noname00 scripts]$ sh hello_world.sh
    Hello World
    [user1@noname00 scripts]$ ksh hello_world.sh
    Hello World
    [user1@noname00 scripts]$

- Assigning permissions of execution to the file and writing symbols "./" before the name of the script:

    [user1@noname00 scripts]$ ls -la
    total 8
    drwxrwxr-x 2 user1 user1   26 dic 1 15:23 .
    drwx------ 10 user1 user1 4096 dic 1 15:23 ..
    -rw-rw-r-- 1 user1 user1   16 dic 1 15:23 hello_world.sh
    [user1@noname00 scripts]$ ./hello_world.sh

```
-bash: ./hello_world.sh: Permission denied
[user1@noname00 scripts]$


[user1@noname00 scripts]$ chmod u+x hello_world.sh
[user1@noname00 scripts]$ ./hello_world.sh
Hello World
[user1@noname00 scripts]$
```

- If the script contains environment variables we will write ". " (a point followed by a space) abd the name of the file,in order to preserve the value of the variables within our user session. We get the same result with the command "export Variable=Value".

    Example:

    ```
    [user1@noname00 scripts]$ cat variables.sh
    NAME=David
    [user1@noname00 scripts]$ ./variables.sh
    [user1@noname00 scripts]$ echo $NAME

    [user1@noname00 scripts]$ . variables.sh
    [user1@noname00 scripts]$ echo $NAME
    David
    [user1@noname00 scripts]$
    ```

    As we can see, with the command ". variables.sh " yes we get the value of the variable *NAME*, writing the symbol "$" before the variable name.

    This function will be useful to us for not having to load manually the environment variables that need a software to run, for example, we could load the variable *JAVA_HOME* for a program written in Java or load the variable *SID* to work with an Oracle database.

Reserved variables

There are a number of variables reserved by the shell for a specific use. They are:

\# → Saves the number of parameters associated with the execution of the script.
* → Save the string of arguments.
? → Save the error code returned by the last order of the script (0 = No errors).
@ → Saves the entire string of parameters but as a list of strings and not as one only.
$0 → It is not really a reserved variable, but represents the first field in the line of argument, which is the name of the script.

Example:

- Contents of the script:

    ```
    [user1@noname00 scripts]$ cat parameters.sh
    #!/bin/bash

    PARAMETER1=$1
    PARAMETER2=$2
    PARAMETER3=$3
    ARRAY_PARAMETERS=$@
    TIME=$(date)

    echo The value of parameter1 is: $PARAMETER1
    echo The value of parameter2 is: $PARAMETER2
    echo The value of parameter3 is: $PARAMETER3

    echo The error code returned by the last command of the script has been: $?

    echo The number of parameters associated with this script are: $#

    echo The parameters that are passed are: $*

    echo We attach a command to a variable, which gives us the current time: $TIME
    [user1@noname00 scripts]$
    ```

- Execution:

    ```
    [user1@noname00 scripts]$ ./parameters.sh param1 param2 param3
    ```

The value of parameter1 is: param1
The value of parameter2 is: param2
The value of parameter3 is: param3
The error code returned by the last command of the script has been: 0
The number of parameters associated with this script are: 3
The parameters that are passed are: param1 param2 param3
We attach a command to a variable, which gives us the current time: lun dic 1 16:22:54 CET 2008

Functions of the shell

shift *number*

It is used for the value of a parameter is equivalent to that at the current position more *number*, that is, if *number* is **2**, the parameter number **1** will be equal to the value of the parameter that is in position **3 (1+2)**.

Example:

```
[user1@noname00 scripts]$ cat shift.sh
#!/bin/bash
echo Original values of the parameters:
echo The value of the parameter ONE is:  $1
echo The value of the parameter  TWO is: $2
echo The value of the parameter  THREE is:  $3
shift 2
echo Values of the parameters after the use of the shift command:
echo \$1 is: $1
echo \$2 is: $2
echo \$3 is: $3
[user1@noname00 scripts]$


[user1@noname00 scripts]$ ./shift.sh ONE TWO THREE FOUR FIVE
Original values of the parameters:
```

The value of the parameter ONE is: ONE
The value of the parameter TWO is: TWO
The value of the parameter THREE is: THREE
Values of the parameters after the use of the shift command:
$1 is: THREE
$2 is: FOUR
$3 is: FIVE
[user1@noname00 scripts]$

read *variables*

It serves to store the value of one or more variables that we have entered via the keyboard.

Example:

- Contents of the script:

    ```
    [user1@noname00 scripts]$ cat read.sh
    #!/bin/ksh

    echo Enter your name:
    read Name
    echo Write your last name:
    read LastName1 LastName2
    echo
    echo Your full name is: $Name $LastName1 $LastName2
    [user1@noname00 scripts]$
    ```

- Execution:

    ```
    [user1@noname00 scripts]$ ./read.sh
    Enter your name:
    David
    Write your last name:
    ```

```
Martínez Perales
Your full name is: David Martínez Perales
[user1@noname00 scripts]$
```

expr

It is used to make arithmetic operations.

Arithmetic Operators	
+	Sum
-	Subtraction
*	Multiplication Note: This symbol also corresponds with a special variable for the shell, so if we want to use it as multiplication, it will have to write as "\ *".
/	Division
%	Rest of the division
Relational operators	
=	Equal
!=	Different
>	Greater than
>=	Greater or equal than
<	Less than
<=	Less or equal than

Logical Operators	
| (pipe)	OR operation
&	AND operation

Example:

    [user1@noname00 ~]$ expr 15 + 30
    45
    [user1@noname00 ~]$

test

Evaluates two expressions. Below is a description of its arguments:

- Parameters related to the files:

    -f → Returns 0 if the file exists and is neither a directory or a device.
    -s → Returns 0 if the file exists and has a size greater than 0.
    -r → Returns 0 if the file exists and has read permission.
    -w → Returns 0 if the file exists and has write permission.
    -d → Returns 0 if the search belongs to a directory.

- Parameters related to the text strings:

    -z → Returns 0 if the number of characters in a string is equal to 0.
    -n → Like the previous parameter with the difference that verifies that the size of the string is greater than 0.

- Parameters related to numbers:

    -lt → Less than
    -le → Less or equal than
    -gt → Greater than
    -ge → Greater or equal than

-eq → Equal to
-ne → Different of

A simple example of using this function:

> Contents of the script:

    [user1@noname00 scripts]$ cat testsc.sh
    #!/bin/bash

    echo -n "We are going to verify that the file testsc.sh exists: "

    test -f "testsc.sh"

    echo $?

    STRING="I am a text string"

    echo -n "We are going to see see if the string is empty: "

    test -z "$STRING"

    echo $?

    NUM1=10
    NUM2=20

    echo -n "We are going to see if NUM1 is greater than NUM2: "

    test $NUM1 -gt $NUM2

    echo $?
    [user1@noname00 scripts]$

> Execution:

    [user1@noname00 scripts]$ ./testsc.sh

We are going to verify that the file testsc.sh exists: 0
We are going to see see if the string is empty: 1
We are going to see if NUM1 is greater than NUM2: 1
[user1@noname00 scripts]$

if

It is used to perform a task or another depending on whether fulfilled or is not a condition.

Example:

- Contents of the script:

    ```
    [user1@noname00 scripts]$ cat ifsc.sh
    #!/bin/bash

    # We check if is listening the port 80, typical of a Web server
    WS=`netstat -an |grep " 80 " |grep LISTEN`

    # If the string is empty
    if [[ -z $WS ]]
    then

        echo We have no service started and listening on port 80.

    else

        echo We have started a Webserver

    fi
    [user1@noname00 scripts]$
    ```

- Execution:

    ```
    [user1@noname00 scripts]$ ./ifsc.sh
    We have no service started and listening on port 80.
    ```

[user1@noname00 scripts]$

case

Compare the value of a variable with the values defined in each of the estates.

Syntax:

    case *variable* in
        estate1) Actions to execute;;
        estate2) Actions to execute;;
        estate "n") Actions to execute;;
    esac

Example:

- Contents of the script:

```
[user1@noname00 scripts]$ cat casesc.sh
#!/bin/bash

echo Write a number 1 through 3:
read NUM

case $NUM in

    1) echo You have entered the number 1;;
    2) echo You have entered the number 2;;
    3) echo You have entered the number 3;;
    *) echo The number or the written word does not match the range requested;;

esac
[user1@noname00 scripts]$
```

- Execution:

```
[user1@noname00 scripts]$ ./casesc.sh
Write a number 1 through 3:
2
You have entered the number 2
[user1@noname00 scripts]$ ./casesc.sh
Write a number 1 through3:
5
he number or the written word does not match the range requested
[user1@noname00 scripts]$
```

while

The actions are executing while enforcing a condition.

Syntax:

```
while condition
do

    actions

done
```
Example:

- We have the directory *files* with the following contents:

    ```
    [user1@noname00 scripts]$ cd files/
    [user1@noname00 files]$ ls -la
    total 40
    drwxrwxr-x 2 user1 user1  140 dic  2 19:04 .
    drwxrwxr-x 3 user1 user1 4096 dic  2 19:04 ..
    -rwxrw-r-- 1 user1 user1  275 dic  2 19:04 casesc.sh
    -rwxrw-r-- 1 user1 user1   16 dic  2 19:04 hello_world.sh
    -rwxrw-r-- 1 user1 user1  206 dic  2 19:04 ifsc.sh
    -rwxrw-r-- 1 user1 user1  493 dic  2 19:04 parameters.sh
    -rwxrwxr-x 1 user1 user1  165 dic  2 19:04 read.sh
    ```

```
-rwxrw-r-- 1 user1 user1  317 dic  2 19:04 shift.sh
-rwxrw-r-- 1 user1 user1  341 dic  2 19:04 testsc.sh
-rwxrw-r-- 1 user1 user1   13 dic  2 19:04 variables.sh
[user1@noname00 files]$
```

➢ We create a script for packaging some files in tar format:

```
[user1@noname00 scripts]$ cat whilesc.sh
#!/bin/bash

while read FILE
do

    echo "Packing the file $FILE" \n
    tar cvf $FILE.tar $FILE

done <<EOF
files/casesc.sh
files/hello_world.sh
files/variables.sh
EOF
[user1@noname00 scripts]$
```

➢ We execute it:

```
[user1@noname00 scripts]$ ./whilesc.sh
Packing the file files/casesc.sh n
files/casesc.sh
Packing the file files/hello_world.sh n
files/hello_world.sh
Packing the file files/variables.sh n
files/variables.sh
[user1@noname00 scripts]$
```

➢ We check that has packaged the files that we wanted:

```
[user1@noname00 files]$ ls -la
total 80
drwxrwxr-x 2 user1 user1  4096 dic  2 19:10 .
drwxrwxr-x 3 user1 user1  4096 dic  2 19:10 ..
```

```
-rwxrw-r-- 1 user1 user1   275 dic  2 19:04 casesc.sh
-rw-rw-r-- 1 user1 user1 10240 dic  2 19:10 casesc.sh.tar
-rwxrw-r-- 1 user1 user1    16 dic  2 19:04 hello_world.sh
-rw-rw-r-- 1 user1 user1 10240 dic  2 19:10 hello_world.sh.tar
-rwxrw-r-- 1 user1 user1   206 dic  2 19:04 ifsc.sh
-rwxrw-r-- 1 user1 user1   493 dic  2 19:04 parameters.sh
-rwxrwxr-x 1 user1 user1   165 dic  2 19:04 read.sh
-rwxrw-r-- 1 user1 user1   317 dic  2 19:04 shift.sh
-rwxrw-r-- 1 user1 user1   341 dic  2 19:04 testsc.sh
-rwxrw-r-- 1 user1 user1    13 dic  2 19:04 variables.sh
-rw-rw-r-- 1 user1 user1 10240 dic  2 19:10 variables.sh.tar
[user1@noname00 files]$
```

Now, we are going to read the contents of a file:

```
while read line
do

    echo $line

done < myfile.txt
```

until

The orders are executed until enforcing a condition.

Syntax:

```
until condition
do

    actions

done
```

for

Are run a series of commands until finishes the read of a list.

Syntax:

> for *variable* in *list*
> do
>
> > *actions*
>
> done

Example of a sequential use:

- Content of the script:

    [user1@noname00 scripts]$ cat forex.sh
    #!/bin/bash

    for i in `seq 1 10`; do

      echo the value of the variable i is: $i

    done
    [user1@noname00 scripts]$

- Execution of script:

    [user1@noname00 scripts]$ ./forex.sh
    the value of the variable i is: 1
    the value of the variable i is: 2
    the value of the variable i is: 3
    the value of the variable i is: 4
    the value of the variable i is: 5
    the value of the variable i is: 6
    the value of the variable i is: 7
    the value of the variable i is: 8
    the value of the variable i is: 9
    the value of the variable i is: 10
    [user1@noname00 scripts]$

➢ Contents of script:

```
[user1@noname00 scripts]$ cat forsc.sh
#!/bin/bash
# We look for all files with extension "sh" in the directory "files"
for F in `find files -name "*.sh"`
do

   # Compress all files found
   echo Compressing in gzip the file $F
   gzip $F

done
[user1@noname00 scripts]$
```

➢ Execution of script:

```
[user1@noname00 scripts]$ ./forsc.sh
Compressing in gzip the file files/casesc.sh
Compressing in gzip the file files/hello_world.sh
Compressing in gzip the file files/ifsc.sh
Compressing in gzip the file files/parameters.sh
Compressing in gzip the file files/read.sh
Compressing in gzip the file files/shift.sh
Compressing in gzip the file files/testsc.sh
Compressing in gzip the file files/variables.sh
[user1@noname00 scripts]$
```

➢ We check the result:

```
[user1@noname00 files]$ ls -al
total 80
drwxrwxr-x 2 user1 user1  4096 dic  2 19:28 .
drwxrwxr-x 3 user1 user1  4096 dic  2 19:28 ..
-rwxrw-r-- 1 user1 user1   184 dic  2 19:04 casesc.sh.gz
```

```
-rw-rw-r-- 1 user1 user1 10240 dic  2 19:18 casesc.sh.tar
-rwxrw-r-- 1 user1 user1    50 dic  2 19:04 hello_world.sh.gz
-rw-rw-r-- 1 user1 user1 10240 dic  2 19:18 hello_world.sh.tar
-rwxrw-r-- 1 user1 user1   186 dic  2 19:04 ifsc.sh.gz
-rwxrw-r-- 1 user1 user1   301 dic  2 19:04 parameters.sh.gz
-rwxrwxr-x 1 user1 user1   126 dic  2 19:04 read.sh.gz
-rwxrw-r-- 1 user1 user1   191 dic  2 19:04 shift.sh.gz
-rwxrw-r-- 1 user1 user1   216 dic  2 19:04 testsc.sh.gz
-rwxrw-r-- 1 user1 user1    46 dic  2 19:04 variables.sh.gz
-rw-rw-r-- 1 user1 user1 10240 dic  2 19:18 variables.sh.tar
[user1@noname00 files]$
```

break, continue and exit

The three commands are used to interrupt a loop for, while o until.

- **break**: We leave the loop completely and continue with the execution of the script.
- **continue:** We leave the current implementation of the loop but continue with the next repetition.
- **exit *n*:** Stops the execution of the script and assigns to *n* the error code.

Example:

- Content of the script:

```
[user1@noname00 scripts]$ cat loop.sh
#!/bin/bash
for i in 1 2 3 4 5
do

   if [[ $i = 3 ]]
   then

      # If number is 3, jump to the next iteration of the loop

      continue
```

```
        else
            echo $i
        fi
done
```

➢ Execution:

```
[user1@noname00 scripts]$ sh loop.sh
1
2
4
5
[user1@noname00 scripts]$
```

select

It serves to create a menu of options.

Example:

➢ Contents of the script:

```
[user1@noname00 scripts]$ cat selectsc.sh
#!/bin/bash

echo Choose an option:
echo lsla – Executes the command "ls -la".
echo whor - Executes the command "who -r".
echo Exit

PS3="Option: "
select i in lsla whor Exit
do
   case $i in
```

```
        lsla) ls -la;;
        whor) who -r;;
        Exit) exit 0;;
        *) {

        clear
        echo "1) lsla"
        echo "2) whor"
        echo "3) Exit"
      }

    esac

done
[user1@noname00 scripts]$
```

- Execution:

```
[user1@noname00 scripts]$ ./selectsc.sh
Choose an option:
lsla - Executes the command ls -la.
whor - Executes the command who -r.
Exit
1) lsla
2) whor
3) Exit
Option: 1
total 60
drwxrwxr-x  3 user1 user1 4096 dic  2 19:45 .
drwx------ 10 user1 user1 4096 dic  2 19:45 ..
-rwxrw-r--  1 user1 user1  275 dic  1 18:12 casesc.sh
drwxrwxr-x  2 user1 user1 4096 dic  2 19:28 files
-rwxrw-r--  1 user1 user1  116 dic  2 19:28 forsc.sh
-rwxrw-r--  1 user1 user1   16 dic  1 15:23 hello_world.sh
-rwxrw-r--  1 user1 user1  206 dic  1 18:01 ifsc.sh
-rwxrw-r--  1 user1 user1  493 dic  1 16:22 parameters.sh
-rwxrwxr-x  1 user1 user1  165 dic  1 17:07 read.sh
-rwxrw-r--  1 user1 user1  397 dic  2 19:45 selectsc.sh
-rwxrw-r--  1 user1 user1  317 dic  1 16:51 shift.sh
-rwxrw-r--  1 user1 user1  341 dic  1 17:54 testsc.sh
```

```
-rwxrw-r--  1 user1 user1   13 dic  1 15:32 variables.sh
-rwxrw-r--  1 user1 user1  193 dic  2 19:19 whilesc.sh
Option: 2
        `run-level' 5 2008-12-21 07:20
Option: 3
[user1@noname00 scripts]$
```

Use of arrays

An array is a group of variables to which access is by index. Here is an example of usage:

- Content of the script:

    ```
    [user1@noname00 scripts]$ cat array.sh
    #!/bin/bash

    myarray=(red green blue)

    echo Value in the first position in the array: ${myarray[0]}
    echo Value in the second position in the array: ${myarray[1]}
    echo Value in the third position in the array: ${myarray[2]}
    [user1@noname00 scripts]$
    ```

- Execution of the script:

    ```
    [user1@noname00 scripts]$ ./array.sh
    Value in the first position in the array: red
    Value in the second position in the array: green
    Value in the third position in the array: blue
    [user1@noname00 scripts]$
    ```

We may also use the variable "set" to group the variables. It works as follows:

- Content of the script:

```
[user1@noname00 scripts]$ cat NameServers.sh
#!/sbin/sh

set -A SRVS "Server1 Servrer2 Server3 Server4"

for SERVER in ${SRVS}
do

    echo $SERVER

done
[user1@noname00 scripts]$
```

> Execution of the script:

```
[user1@noname00 scripts]$ ./NameServers.sh
Server1
Server2
Server3
Server4
[user1@noname00 scripts]$
```

Functions created by us

The functions are used to run the code contained when they are called, in this way we avoid writing the same code each time we need it.
Syntax:

Function definition

function *Function_Name* {

    Orders

}

The function is called from the script

Function_Name

Example:

> Contents of the script:

```
[user1@noname00 scripts]$ cat function.sh
#!/bin/bash

# Function definition

function unlock_account () {

   # This function unlocks a user account

   # USER takes the value of the first parameter that is passed to the function
   USER=$1

   # Unlock the account
   passwd -u $USER

}


# Body of the script

echo
echo "Enter the user account you want to unlock:"
read ACCOUNT

unlock_account $ACCOUNT

RESULT=$?

if [[ $RESULT = 0 ]]
then

    echo The account has been successfully unlocked.
```

```
        else

            echo Unable to unlock the account.

        fi

        echo
        [user1@noname00 scripts]$
```

> Execution failed to check the condition defined in section "if – fi":

```
[user1@noname00 scripts]$ ./function.sh

Enter the user account you want to unlock:
David
Only root can do that.
Unable to unlock the account.

[user1@noname00 scripts]$
```

> Execution successful:

```
[root@noname00 scripts]# ./function.sh

Enter the user account you want to unlock:
user1
Unlocking the password for the user user1.
passwd: Successful
The account has been successfully unlocked.

[root@noname00 scripts]#
```

If we want grouping a number of functions in a single file (library), from our script can load this file, as follows:
        . /libraries/libraries_file.lib

Following this definition we can make a call to the functions defined in this file.

Example:

- ➤ We create the library:

    ```
    [root@noname00 scripts]# cat function.lib
    #!/bin/bash

    function unlock_account () {

      # This function unlocks a user account

      USER=$1

      passwd -u $USER

    }
    ```

- ➤ We create the script that uses the library functions:

    ```
    [root@noname00 scripts]#
    [root@noname00 scripts]# cat function2.sh
    #!/bin/bash
    ```

    . function.lib

    ```
    echo
    echo "Enter the user account you want to unlock"
    read ACCOUNT
    ```

    unlock_account $ACCOUNT

    ```
    RESULT=$?

    if [[ $RESUL = 0 ]]
    then

        echo The account has been successfully unlocked.
    ```

else

   echo Unable to unlock the account.

fi

echo
[root@noname00 scripts]#

➤ We execute the script:

[root@noname00 scripts]# ./function2.sh

Enter the user account you want to unlock:
user1
Unlocking the password for the user user1.
passwd:
The account has been successfully unlocked.

[root@noname00 scripts]#

Save useful information generated by a script

When we are programming a script, it is very likely that we want to save the information generated to view it after its execution, to keep it as a historical, to compare it, because another script will need, etc. To store the information in a file, as general rule, we will use the redirect methods were explained in the chapter "Modify the standard output of a command", however, exists a specific command to store the information in the system log. This command is called "logger" and works as follows:

[root@noname00 scripts]# *pwd*
/var/log
[root@noname00 scripts]# ***logger*** *"Test message to store in the system log"*
[root@noname00 scripts]# *tail -1 messages*
Apr 16 09:52:09 noname00 *user1: Test message to store in the system log*

[root@noname00 scripts]#

However, it may not always store the information we are interested in the system log. In fact, it is not usual. Normally whould be to store it in a specific log file for each script.

For example:

- We save the script information in the file /tmp/milog.log-

    [root@noname00 scripts]# sh miscript.sh > /tmp/milog.log

- Now, we save the script information and the commands it call.

    [root@noname00 scripts]# sh miscript.sh > /tmp/milog.log *2>&1*

High availability systems

Concepts

A high availability system (HA) consists in that the service being given, is sufficiently backed so that could never be interrupted, even in case of incidence.

The characteristics of this type of service are as follows:

- The power supply that supplies the computer equipment has to be supplied by two different companies because in the event of a breakdown in one of them, we can always get energy from the other.
- Even if both companies fail, the CPD (Data Processing Center) must be powered by an UPS (Uninterrupted Power Supply), which will ensure electricity supply over a reasonable period in which we can close, orderly, the systems and applications if the damage is too big as for can not solve it fast enough.
- The computers must have two power supplies as a minimum, each connected to an outlet different for that the hardware continue to have electricity if it breaks down some or there is any fault in one of the outlets.
- Network cards and hard drives also have to be Redundant. We can connect two network cards to serve a single IP, so if a card is damaged, we will continue having service on the other. For hard drives, those containing the data must be external disks.
- The servers that make up the cluster, for more security, must be physically located in different CPD and in different tectonic plates.
- As for the software:

    - It always must be configured in cluster.
    - The critical data must be stored in a tower of disks that can be accessed by more than one server if the main has a problem.

What is a cluster of applications?

It consists of that a single application can be run in two or more different systems, all of them available for service at any time.
- **Cluster active-active:** All servers serve at once.
- **Cluster active-passive:** A server will provide the service when the principal is not in a position because of any incidence of hardware or software.

Following is an outline of a software environment in cluster:

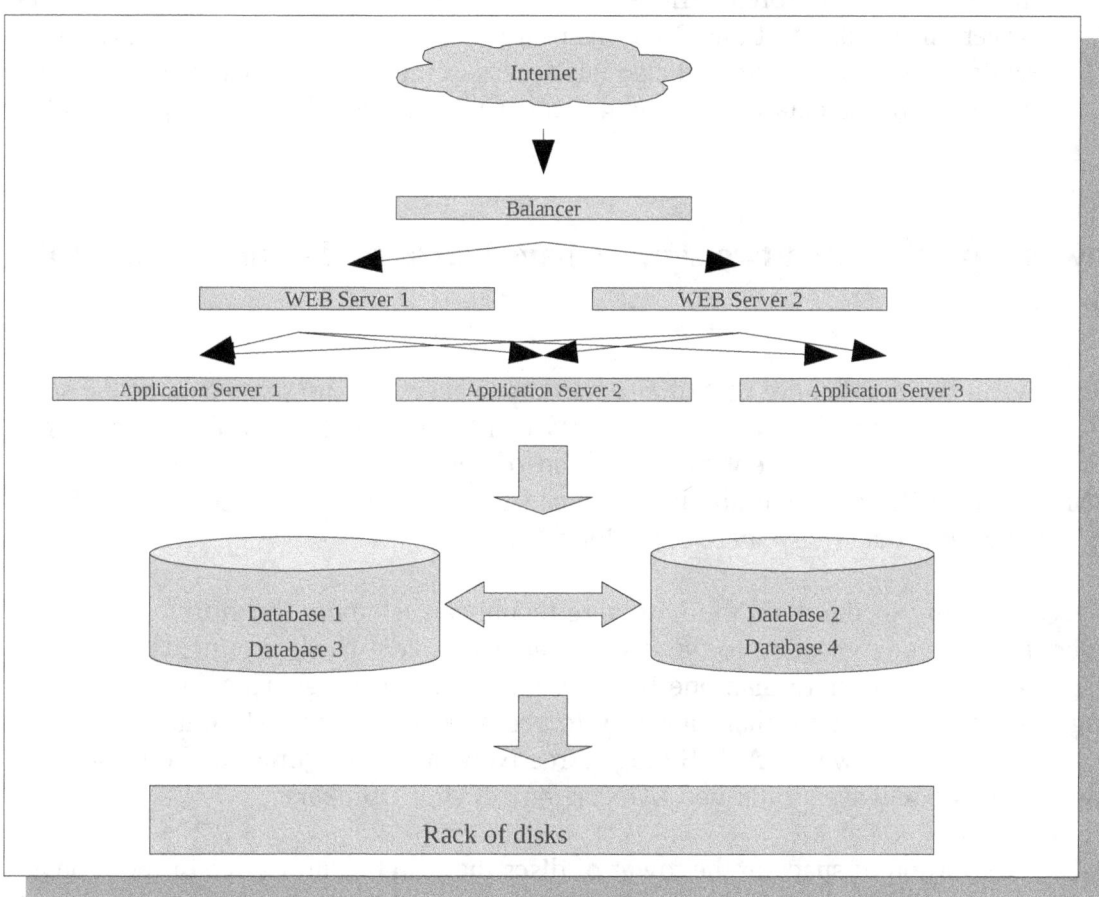

The previous scheme is interpreted as follows:

- An Internet user enters a Web page through its IP public, which resides in the balancer.

- This element is responsible for distributing the load between two WEB servers, which can send the user's request to any of the three application servers available (cluster active-active).
- If fall out any of the application servers, the webservers could still send the requests to the other two remaining.
- The application needs to consult, write or erase some data from the databases located on the two servers, as we can see. The first contains databases "1" and "3", while in the second contains the number 2 and number 4. Each database is independent and stores different information, however, if falls out the first server, the databases 1 and 3 will can start in the second, because there resides a replica of startup scripts and also has access to the rack of disks. The same thing happen with the databases 2 and 4. This is what is called an active-passive cluster.

How is it possible that two servers have access to the same disks of the tower?

Normally, all servers that are part of a service have access to the same data of the same disks at the same time, but a filesystem only can be mounted in a only one server to prevent data corruption, except in some kind of services and filesystems like Oracle ASM or RedHat GFS, which are automanaged for all servers can access at the "same time" to the same data (they share data blocks).

To give visibility to the disk, the hardware tecnhician, connect the fiber cables to all servers must have connection to the disk tower. To prevent hardware incidents, the cables are connected to more than one fiber card of the each server. This means the operating system will see more than one way to access to the same disk. Once completed the hardware and software SAN (Storage Area Network) configuration, from the operating system we will see all defined LUNs (Logical Unit Number).

A LUN is a portion of space in the tower of discs that can be part of one or more physical disks. From the operating system all LUNs are treated as if they were unique physical disks.

According to the wiring of the chart on the next page, servers 1 and 2, will see the same disk by four different paths since there are two cards fibers in the tower and two in each server.

The software that came with the tower allows us to visualize each of the LUNs and configure the *multipathing*, that is, distributing access from UNIX servers to the tower by different paths and, therefore, optimizing the response times of reading and writing on disks and providing greater security and robustness to the system..

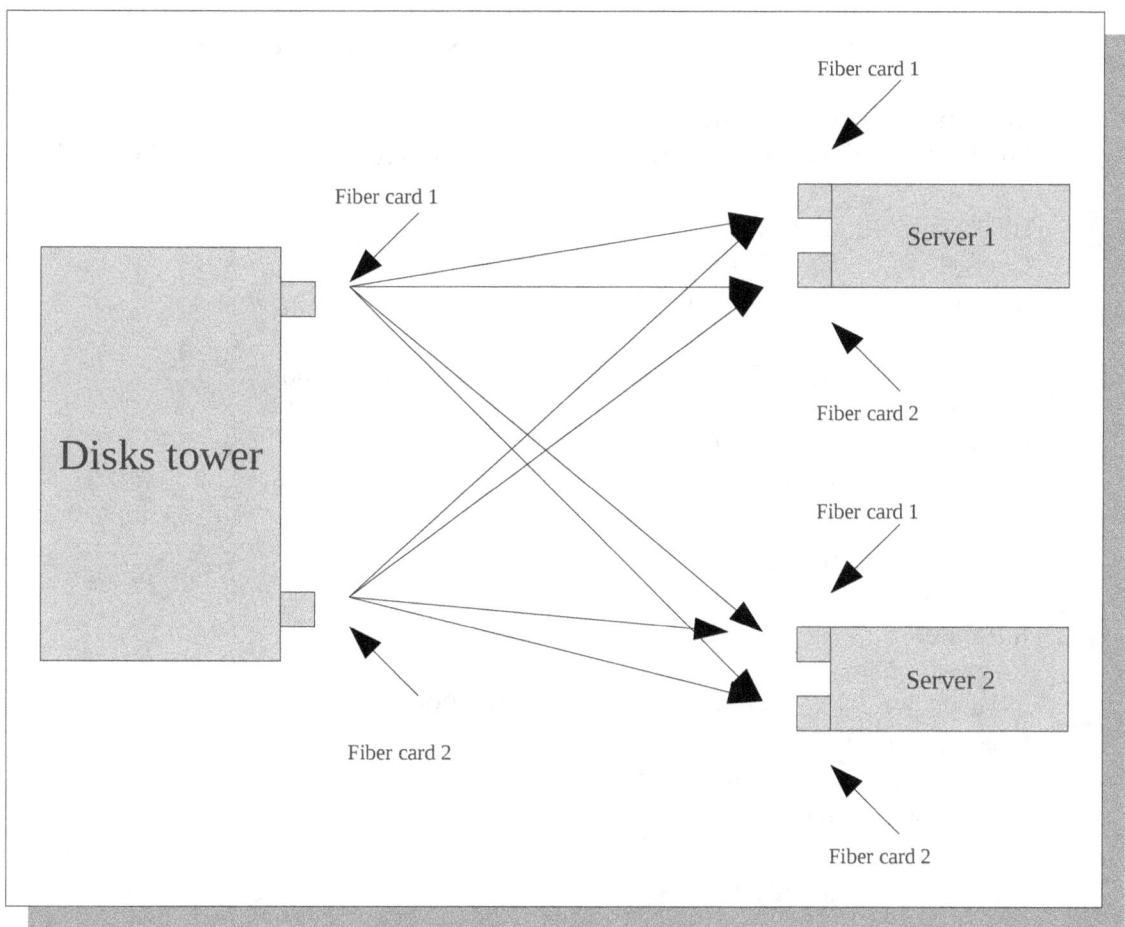

Really, the above scheme is not totally true, becaouse in the tower side, usually exist different fiber switch, also redundat, with access to the same disk. There fore, may increase the number of paths we see from the operating system. The hardware architecture can be complicated or securize much as we wish. The important thing is to have understood the concept.

Formerly, the SAN manufacturers develop their own multipath software for each different operating system. Although they continue developing this kind of software, the modern operating system incorporate its own multipath software. We can see an example on HP-UX 11.31:

```
[noname00] root:/root # scsimgr lun_map -D /dev/rdisk/disk332

      LUN PATH INFORMATION FOR LUN : /dev/rdisk/disk332

Total number of LUN paths   = 8
World Wide Identifier(WWID) = 0x600508b4000cee0600006000091c0000

LUN path : lunpath216
Class              = lunpath
Instance           = 216
Hardware path      =
0/0/14/1/0/4/0.0x50001fe150262259.0x4018000000000000
SCSI transport protocol    = fibre_channel
State              = ACTIVE
Last Open or Close state   = ACTIVE

LUN path : lunpath225
Class              = lunpath
Instance           = 225
Hardware path      =
0/0/14/1/0/4/0.0x50001fe15026225b.0x4018000000000000
SCSI transport protocol    = fibre_channel
State              = ACTIVE
Last Open or Close state   = ACTIVE

LUN path : lunpath219
Class              = lunpath
Instance           = 219
Hardware path      =
0/0/14/1/0/4/0.0x50001fe15026225d.0x4018000000000000
SCSI transport protocol    = fibre_channel
State              = STANDBY
Last Open or Close state   = STANDBY
```

LUN path : lunpath218
Class   = lunpath
Instance   = 218
Hardware path   =
0/0/14/1/0/4/0.0x50001fe15026225f.0x4018000000000000
SCSI transport protocol   = fibre_channel
State   = STANDBY
Last Open or Close state   = STANDBY

LUN path : lunpath220
Class   = lunpath
Instance   = 220
Hardware path   =
1/0/14/1/0/4/0.0x50001fe15026225c.0x4018000000000000
SCSI transport protocol   = fibre_channel
State   = STANDBY
Last Open or Close state   = STANDBY

LUN path : lunpath221
Class   = lunpath
Instance   = 221
Hardware path   =
1/0/14/1/0/4/0.0x50001fe15026225e.0x4018000000000000
SCSI transport protocol   = fibre_channel
State   = STANDBY
Last Open or Close state   = STANDBY

LUN path : lunpath217
Class   = lunpath
Instance   = 217
Hardware path   =
1/0/14/1/0/4/0.0x50001fe150262258.0x4018000000000000
SCSI transport protocol   = fibre_channel
State   = ACTIVE
Last Open or Close state   = ACTIVE

LUN path : lunpath224
Class   = lunpath
Instance   = 224

```
Hardware path              =
1/0/14/1/0/4/0.0x50001fe15026225a.0x4018000000000000
SCSI transport protocol    = fibre_channel
State                      = ACTIVE
Last Open or Close state   = ACTIVE

[noname00] root:/root #
```

With above command we now the operating system has access to the disk332 disk thought eight different paths, as we can see in the field "Total number of LUN paths".

Configuring a cluster

In the market there are many cluster tools such as Veritas Cluster or Service Guard, to cite some of the most used. In order to understand the concepts explained above, with a real software, we will use Service Guard. It should not be taken at exactly the configuration we do then, as there are several different modules and extensions of specific products and, as is well known, the world of computers and applications is constantly evolving, so that in future versions, can change the method or manner of product configuration.

Service Guard is a utility to pay Hewlett-Packard available for different UNIX environments and, to explain the concepts of cluster, we will use the version A.11.17.00. Although we know there are newer versions in the market, this will be very graphic to understand how works a software cluster.

- We start from the premise that the filesystems that use the cluster are created and they use the tower of discs so that we can start the service in the backup system if the main falls. In this example we will use the structure LVM and all servers that are part of the cluster should have the information of the VGs to use, that is, previously has been executed the command *vgimport* in each server.

- The next step is to create the information of the cluster (name, nodes in it, etc.). To do this we will go to the directory */etc/cmcluster* and we will edit the file *cmclconfig.asci*i as follows:

    # Name of the cluster

```
CLUSTER_NAME              MY_CLUSTER


# Cluster lock disk
FIRST_CLUSTER_LOCK_VG            /dev/vgclkp

# We configure the network of the server "server1"
NODE_NAME                 server1
NETWORK_INTERFACE    lan5
HEARTBEAT_IP      172.23.66.13
# Standby Interface
NETWORK_INTERFACE    lan1
# Heartbeat interface
 NETWORK_INTERFACE    lan4
HEARTBEAT_IP      1.1.1.10
FIRST_CLUSTER_LOCK_PV        /dev/dsk/c14t0d0 /dev/dsk/c15t0d0
/dev/dsk/c12t0d0 /dev/dsk/c13t0d0


# We configure the network of the server  "server2"
NODE_NAME                 server2
NETWORK_INTERFACE    lan3
HEARTBEAT_IP      172.23.66.14
# Standby interface
NETWORK_INTERFACE    lan8
# Heartbeat interface
NETWORK_INTERFACE    lan4
HEARTBEAT_IP       1.1.1.11


FIRST_CLUSTER_LOCK_PV       /dev/dsk/c8t0d0        /dev/dsk/c9t0d0
/dev/dsk/c10t0d0 /dev/dsk/c11t0d0


HEARTBEAT_INTERVAL           1000000
NODE_TIMEOUT             2000000

AUTO_START_TIMEOUT  600000000
NETWORK_POLLING_INTERVAL         2000000
NETWORK_FAILURE_DETECTION            INOUT
```

MAX_CONFIGURED_PACKAGES   150

VOLUME_GROUP   /dev/myvg

The meaning of some of the most important parameters of this file is:
- **Network interface:** It is the primary network which will use each server to communicate.
- **Heartbeat IP:** It is a network interface used for all nodes in the cluster to communicate with each other over the network. They are usually set up two interfaces HeartBeat, in anticipation of an unavailability of the first.
- Cluster lock: It is a disk that has to be accessible by all nodes in the cluster. Allows us to know the status of each package, at every moment, and knowing where it must be started. When a node takes control of the cluster lock, the rest acknowledge that fact. The disk may be a LVM VG unique to this function and should appear as deactivated during the operation of the service, although it will be activated, momentarily, at the time of compiling the binary of the cluster. Is important that the file cmclconfig.ascii has properly configured this disk, because if there is a problem with the HEARBEAT IP visibility and there is not configured the clusterlock disk, all the servers that make up the cluster will think that they are isolated and we can suffer a crash in all these systems, because it can not communicate with each other.

- Then, we will configure the packages that may switch between each of the systems. With the command *cmmakepkg –p Package_name.conf*, we can create a template (in */etc/cmcluster*) and then change depending on the structure of the package we need.

The services that are included must have a virtual IP which can switch with the package, because a service always will listen by the same IP, regardless of the server where is started.

In the file *.conf*, we have the package name and order that sets the primary server and the backup:

[server1] root:/etc/cmcluster/pkgcmsd # cat mypkg.conf

```
PACKAGE_NAME            mypkg
PACKAGE_TYPE            FAILOVER
FAILOVER_POLICY           CONFIGURED_NODE
FAILBACK_POLICY           MANUAL

# Primary server
NODE_NAME     server1

# Backup server
NODE_NAME     server2

AUTO_RUN                  YES
LOCAL_LAN_FAILOVER_ALLOWED     YES
NODE_FAIL_FAST_ENABLED         NO

# File with the scripts that run during the startup of the package
RUN_SCRIPT     /etc/cmcluster/mypkg/mypkg.ctl
RUN_SCRIPT_TIMEOUT        NO_TIMEOUT

# File with the scripts that run during the stop of the package
HALT_SCRIPT    /etc/cmcluster/mypkg/mypkg.ctl
HALT_SCRIPT_TIMEOUT       NO_TIMEOUT
SUBNET 172.23.66.0
```

On the server "server2" there is an exact copy of this file.

- Then, we will configure the file mypkg.ctl to start and stop the applications during startup and shut-down of the package:

```
[server1] root:/etc/cmcluster/mypkgpkg # cat mypkg.ctl

. ${SGCONFFILE:=/etc/cmcluster.conf}
PATH=$SGSBIN:/usr/bin:/usr/sbin:/etc:/bin
CVM_ACTIVATION_CMD="vxdg -g \$DiskGroup set
activation=exclusivewrite"

# We define the VGs and filesystems which use this package
VG[0]="myvg"
```

```
DEACTIVATION_RETRY_COUNT=0
KILL_PROCESSES_ACCESSING_RAW_DEVICES="NO"
LV[0]=/dev/myvg/lvol1     FS[0]=/database/MyBD FS_MOUNT_OPT[0]="-o rw"
LV[1]=/dev/myvg/lvol2     FS[1]=/database/MyBD/archivers FS_MOUNT_OPT[1]="-o rw"

# We define the scripts that run during the startup of the package
log_file=${SG_SCRIPT_LOG_FILE:-$0.log}
function customer_defined_run_cmds
{
    /scripts/oracle/startBD.sh
    /scripts/oracle/startListener.sh
    test_return 51
}



# We define the scripts that run during the stop of the package
function customer_defined_halt_cmds
{
# ADD customer defined halt commands.
: # do nothing instruction, because a function must contain some command.

# Stop database Oracle

    /scripts/oracle/stopListener.sh
    /scripts/oracle/stopBD.sh

}
```

- We check the configuration of the cluster with the command

    /usr/sbin/cmcheckconf -T 6 -v -C /etc/cmcluster/cmclconfig.ascii -P /etc/cmcluster/mypkg/mypkg.conf

- If everything is okay, we generate and distribute to all nodes, the binary file in the cluster:

    /usr/sbin/cmapplyconf -v -P mypkg

- Now we can start and stop the cluster and its packages:

    - cmruncl → Start the cluster completely.
    - cmhaltcl → Stop the cluster.
    - cmviewcl -v → Display the state of the cluster.
    - cumrunpkg -p mypkg → Start the package *mypkg*.
    - cmhaltpkg -p mypkg → Stop the package.
    - cmrunnode → Start the node in the cluster where we have executed the command.
    - cmhaltnode → Stops the node.

Example:

```
[server1]root:/etc/cmcluster # cmviewcl

CLUSTER         STATUS
MI_CLUSTER      up

  NODE          STATUS      STATE
  server1       up          running
  server2       up          running

    PACKAGE     STATUS      STATE       AUTO_RUN    NODE
    mypkg       up          running     enabled     server1
[server1]root:/etc/cmcluster #
```

Relationship of commands, and other peculiarities between different UNIX systems

Directory Mappings	AIX	FreeBSD	HP-UX	Linux RedHat	Solaris	Tru64
Root filesystem	/ {/dev/hd4}	/ {/dev/ad0s1a}	/ {/dev/vg00/lvol1}	/ {/dev/sda1}	/ {/dev/vx/dsk/rootvol}	/ {/dev/rz0a}
Home Directory	/home {/dev/hd1}		/home {/dev/vg00/lvol4}	/home	/export/home /dev/vx/dsk/home}	
Temporary directory	/tmp {/dev/hd3}		/tmp {/dev/vg00/lvol6}		/tmp /dev/vx/dsk/swapvol}	
USR directory	/usr {/dev/hd2}	/usr {/dev/ad0s1f}	/usr {/dev/vg00/lvol7}		/usr	/usr {/dev/rz0g}
	/var {/dev/hd9var}	/var {/dev/ad0s1e}	/var {/dev/vg00/lvol8}		/var	
Sample configuration files	-		/usr/newconfig			
User	AIX	FreeBSD	HP-UX	Linux	Solaris	Tru64

Accounts				RedHat		
Password files	/etc/passwd /etc/security/passwd	/etc/passwd /etc/master.passwd	/etc/passwd /tcb/files/auth/r/root	/etc/passwd /etc/shadow	/etc/passwd /etc/shadow	/etc/passwd
Groups file	/etc/group /etc/security/group	/etc/group	/etc/group /etc/logingroup	/etc/group	/etc/group	/etc/group
Maximum # of user ID	4294967295	65535	2147483647	65535	2147483647	65535
Allow/Deny remote login	/etc/security/user {rlogin=true}	/etc/ttys {secure}	/etc/securetty {console}	/etc/securetty {ttyp1}	/etc/default/login {CONSOLE=/dev/console}	/etc/securettys {ttyp1}
User nobody's id #	4294967294	65534	-2	99	60001 & 65534(nobody4)	65534
Group nobody's id #	4294967294	65534	-2(nogroup)	99	60002 & 65534(nogroup)	65534
Recover root password	boot from CD/Tape Installation /Maintenance Start Limited Shell getrootfs hdisk0 vi /etc/security/passwd	ok boot -s passwd root	>boot Interact with IPL ? Y ISL>hpux -iS passwd root	{lilo} control-x linux S passwd root {grub} c kernel vmlinuz-2.4.9-13 single ro root=/dev/hda8	boot cdrom -s mkdir /tmp/a mount /dev/c0t0d0s0 /tmp/a vi /tmp/a/etc/shadow	press the HALT Button or (Control-P) >>>boot -fl s lsmbstartup /sbin/bcheckrc passwd root

				initrd /initrd-2.4.9-13.img boot passwd root		
Create new user	mkuser	adduser	useradd	useradd	useradd	useradd
Delete user	rmuser	rmuser	userdel	userdel	userdel	userdel
List users	lsuser -f ALL		logins		logins	
Modify user account	chuser -a		usermod	usermod	usermod	usermod

General Commands	AIX	FreeBSD	HP-UX	Linux RedHat	Solaris	Tru64
Unique host ID	hostid		uname -i	hostid	hostid	hostid
Administrator	smit		sam	linuxconf	admintool	sysman
Performance monitor	top monitor	top	top glance	top	top	top
System activity reporter	sar	sa	sar	sar	sar	/usr/opt/svr4/bin/sar
Virtual Memory statistics	vmstat	vmstat	vmstat	vmstat	vmstat	vmstat
I/O statistics	iostat	iostat	iostat	iostat	iostat	iostat
Error logs	alog -o -t boot errpt	dmesg	dmesg	dmesg	dmesg	uerf -R -o full

Physical RAM	1TB		4TB	64 GB {>2.3.24}	16TB	4TB
Shared Memory	2.75GB		8TB	sysctl kernel.shm max		
Process Data Space	2GB		4GB	900 MB		
Swap device	/dev/hd6	/dev/ad0s1b	/dev/vg00/lvol2	/dev/sda2	/dev/vx/dsk/swapvol	/dev/rz0b
Swap file type	/etc/swapspaces	swap	swap	partition type 82	swap	raw
Display swap size	lsps -a	swapinfo	swapinfo -a	free	swap -l	swapon -s
Activate Swap	swapon -a	swapon -a	swapon -a	swapon -a	swap -a	swapon -a

Printers	**AIX**	**FreeBSD**	**HP-UX**	**Linux RedHat**	**Solaris**	**Tru64**
Printer Queues	/etc/qconfig	/var/spool/print	/etc/lp/interface/*	/var/spool/lpd/lp/*	/etc/lp/interfaces/*	/usr/spool/lpd
Stop LP	stopsrc -s lpd		lpshut	/etc/init.d/lpd stop	/usr/lib/lp/lpshut	/sbin/init.d/lpd stop
Start LP	startsrc -s lpd	lpd	lpsched	/etc/init.d/lpd start	/usr/lib/lp/lpsched	/sbin/init.d/lpd start
Submit print jobs	enq lp lpr qprt	lp	lp	lpr	lp lpr	lp lpr
LP statistics	enq -A lpq lpstat	lpq	lpstat	lpq	lpstat	lpstat

		qchk					
Remove print jobs		cancel lprm qcan enq -x	cancel lprm	cancel	lprm	cancel lprm	cancel lprm
Add printer queue		smit mkpq		lpadmin -p pq	printtool	lpadmin -p pq	lprsetup
Remove Printer queue		smit rmpq		lpadmin -x pq		lpadmin -x pq	lprsetup
Make default printer		export LPDEST= "pq"		lpadmin -d pq		lpadmin -d pq	export PRINTER ="lp"
TCP/IP		**AIX**	**FreeBSD**	**HP-UX**	**Linux RedHat**	**Solaris**	**Tru64**
Network IP configuration		lsattr -E -l inet0	/etc/rc.conf	/etc/rc.config.d/netconf	/etc/sysconfig/network-scripts/	/etc/hostname.* /etc/inet/* /etc/defaultrouter	/etc/rc.config
Hosts IP addresses		/etc/hosts	/etc/hosts	/etc/hosts	/etc/hosts	/etc/inet/hosts	/etc/hosts
Name service switch		/etc/netsvc.conf	/etc/host.conf	/etc/nsswitch.conf	/etc/nsswitch.conf	/etc/nsswitch.conf	/etc/svc.conf
Network parameters		no -a	sysctl	ndd -h	sysctl -a | grep net	ndd /dev/ [tcp|ip] ?	
Routing daemon		gated	routed	gated	routed	in.routed	routed
NIC Configurations		ifconfig -a	ifconfig -a	lanscan -v	ifconfig -a	ifconfig -a	ifconfig -a

Secondary IP Address	ifconfig en0 alias IP	ifconfig xl0 alias IP	ifconfig lan0:1 IP	modprobe ip_alias ifconfig eth0:1 IP	ifconfig hme0:1 IP up	ifconfig ln0 alias
Login prompt	HERALD @ /etc/security/login.cfg		telnetd -b /etc/issue	/etc/issue	BANNER @ /etc/default/telnetd	/etc/issue
Increase the # of pseudo-terminals	odmget -q "attribute=num and uniquetype=pty/pty/pty" PdAt | sed "s/0-64/0-512/" | odmchange -q "attribute=num and uniquetype=pty/pty/pty" -o PdAt chdev -l pty0 -anum=256 -P reboot		rebuild your kernel with these new values NPTY=# NSTRPY=# reboot insf -d ptys -n # insf -d ptym -n # insf -d pts -s # -e -v	cd /dev ./MAKEDEV -v pty	{/etc/system} set pt_cnt = # {SYSV} set npty = # {BSD} {/etc/iu.ap} ptsl 0 # ldterm ttcompat halt boot -r	cd /dev ./MAKEDEV PTY_1
Maximum # of ptys	512		{MAXUSERS}	256	176 {BSD} 3000 {SYSV}	8192
Remote Shell	remsh rsh	rsh	remsh	rsh	rsh	rsh
YP/NIS service	/usr/lib/nets	/usr/sbin/yp	/usr/lib/nets	/sbin/ypbin	/usr/lib/nets	/usr/sbin/yp

binder	vc/yp/ypbind	bind	vc/yp/ypbind	d	vc/yp/ypbind	bind
System Files	**AIX**	**FreeBSD**	**HP-UX**	**Linux RedHat**	**Solaris**	**Tru64**
NFS exported	/etc/exports	/etc/exports	/etc/exports	/etc/exports	/etc/dfs/dfstab /etc/dfs/sharetab	/etc/exports
NFS Client mounted directories	/etc/xtab		/etc/xtab	/var/lib/nfs/xtab	/etc/rmtab	/var/adm/mountdtab
Max File System	128 GB		128 GB	2 TB	1 TB 8000 TB {vxfs}	128 GB {<= 3.2G} 512 GB {>= 4.0} 16 TB {advfs}
Max File Size	64 GB		128 GB	2 GB {512B block size} 8192 GB {8KB block size}	1 TB 2 GB {=<2.5.1}	128 GB {<= 3.2G} 512 GB {>= 4.0} 16 TB {advfs}
Max # File Descriptors	64 K		60~ K	sysctl fs.file-max	64 K	64 K
DISK/LVM Commands	**AIX**	**FreeBSD**	**HP-UX:Disk & filesystem**	**Linux RedHat**	**Solaris**	**Tru64**
Filesystem table	/etc/filesystems	/etc/fstab	/etc/fstab	/etc/fstab	/etc/vfstab	/etc/fstab

Free disk blocks	df -k	df -k	bdf	df -k	df -k	df -k
Device listing	lsdev -C		/sbin/ioscan	cat /proc/devices	sysdef	
Disk information	bootinfo -s hdisk#	fdisk -v ad0	diskinfo /dev/rdsk/c#t#d#	cat /proc/scsi/scsi0/sda/model	format -d c#t#d# format>current format>inquiry	file /dev/rrz0c
Disk Label	lspv -l hdisk#	disklabel ad0	pvdisplay -v /dev/dsk/C#t#d#	fdisk -l	prtvtoc	disklabel -p rz0
LVM Concepts	Partition	sub disk	logical extents	logical extents	sub disk	sub disk
	Volume	Volume	logical volume	logical volume	Volume	Volume
		Plex			Plex	Plex
	Volume group		volume group	volume group	disk group	disk group
Journal Filesystem type	jfs		vxfs	ext3 reiserfs	vxfs	advfs
Default volume group	/dev/rootvg		/dev/vg00		/dev/vx/dsk/rootdg	/dev/vol/rootdg
Display volume group	lsvg -l rootvg		vgdisplay -v vg00	vgdisplay -v	vxprint -l -g rootdg	volprint -l -g rootdg
Modify physical volume	chpv		pvchange	pvchange		
Prepare	mkdev -c		pvcreate	pvcreate	vxdiskadd	voldiskadd

physical disk	disk -l hdisk#					
List physical volume	lspv	vinum ld	pvdisplay	pvdisplay	vxprint -dl	volprint -dl
Remove disk from volume group	reducevg		vgreduce	vgreduce	vxdg rmdisk	voldg rmdisk
Move logical volumes to another physical volumes	migratepv	vinum move -f drive object	pvmove	pvmove	vxassist move	volassist move
Create volume group	mkvg		vgcreate	vgcreate	vxdg init	voldg init
Remove volume group			vgremove	vgremove		
Volume group availability	chvg varyonvg varyoffvg		vgchange	vgchange		
Restore volume group			vgcfgrestore	vgcfgrestore		
Exports volume group	exportvg		vgexport	vgexport	vxdg deport	voldg deport
Imports volume group	importvg		vgimport	vgimport	vxdg import	voldg import
Volume group	lsvg		vgscan	vgscan		

listing						
Change logical volume characteristics	chlv		lvchange	lvchange	vxedit set	voledit set
List logical volume	lslv	vinum lv	lvdisplay	lvdisplay	vxprint -vl	volprint -vl
Make logical volume	mklv		lvcreate	lvcreate	vxassist make	volassist make
Extend logical volume	extendlv		lvextend	lvextend	vxassist growto	volassist growto
Reduce logical volume	**AIX reduce LV**		**lvreduce**	**lvreduce**	**vxassist shrinkto**	**volassist shrinkto**
Remove logical volume	rmlv	vinum rm vol	lvremove	lvremove	vxedit rm	voledit -g rootdg -rf rm vol1
Prepare boot volumes	bootlist -m normal		lvlnboot	lilo	vxbootsetup	
Remove boot volumes			lvrmboot			
Extend File system	chfs -a size=# /mt		extendfs /dev/vg00/lvol8 fsadm -F vxfs -b {LE * 1024} /mt	resize2fs resize_reiserfs	vxva mkfs -M	
Reduce/Split mirrors	rmlvcopy		lvsplit	lvsplit		

257

Merge mirrors			lvmerge	lvmerge		
Create mirrors	mklv -c 2	vinum mirror drive	lvcreate -m 1		vxassist mirror	volassist make vol 100mb mirror=true
Add mirrors	mklvcopy lv 2		lvextend -m 1			
Create striped volumes	mklv -u 3 -S 64K	vinum stripe drive	lvcreate -i 3 -I 64	lvcreate -i 3 -I 64	vxassist make vol 100mb layout=raid5	volassist make vol 100mb layout=stripe
System recovery tape	mksysb -i /dev/rmt0		/opt/ignite/bin/make_recovery			/usr/sys/bin/btcreate
Backup	savevg -i rootvg	vinum saveconfig	fbackup	tar cvf /dev/rst0 /	ufsdump	vdump
Restore	restvg		frecover	tar xvf /dev/rst0	ufsrestore	vrestore
MISC	**AIX**	**FreeBSD**	**HP-UX**	**Linux RedHat**	**SOLARIS**	**Tru64**
Startup script	/etc/rc	/etc/rc	/sbin/rc	/etc/rc.d/rc	/etc/init.d	/sbin/init.d
Kernel	/usr/lib/boot/unix_up	/kernel	/stand/vmunix	/boot/vmlinuz	/kernel/genunix	/vmunix
Kernel Parameters	lsattr -E -l sys0	sysctl -a	sysdef kmtune kmsystem	sysctl -a	sysdef -i	sysconfig dxkerneltuner
Reconfigure the kernel	chdev -l sys0 -a	cd /sys/i386/conf	cd /stand/build	cd /usr/src/linux	vi /etc/system	doconfig

			vi KERNEL config KERNEL cd ../../compile/KERNEL make depend make make install	/usr/lbin/sysadm/system_prep -v -s system vi system mk_kernel -s system cd /stand mv system system.prev mv vmunix vmunix.prev mv dlkm dlkm.prev mv /stand/build/system system kmupdate /stand/build/vmunix_test	make mrproper make menuconfig make dep make clean make bzImage make install make modules make modules_install cp arch/i386/boot/bzImage /boot/vmlinuz-2.2.16 mkinitrd /boot/initrd-2.2.16.img 2.2.16 vi /etc/lilo.conf lilo	reboot	
List modules	genkex		kldstat	kmadmin -s	lsmod	modinfo	
Load module			kldload	kmadmin -L	insmod	modload	
Unload module			kldunload	kmadmin -U	rmmod	modunload	

Initialize system	install_assist	/stand/sysinstall	set_parms initial	netconf	sys-unconfig	netsetup
Physical RAM	bootinfo -r	sysctl hw.physmem	grep -i Physical /var/adm/syslog/syslog.log	free	prtconf	uerf | grep memory
Kernel Bits	bootinfo -K		getconf KERNEL_BITS	getconf LONG_BIT	isainfo -kv	64
Crash utility	crash	crash	adb	lcrash	crash	kdbx
Trace System Calls	syscalls	truss	tusc	strace	truss	trace
Machine model	Uname -m bootinfo -m	uname -m	model uname -m	uname -m	uname -imp	uname -p
OS Level	oslevel	uname -r	uname -r	uname -r	uname -r	sizer -v
Run Level	who -r		who -r	runlevel	who -r	who -r
Core dump files	/var/adm/ras		/var/adm/crash		/var/crash/`uname -n`	
Boot single user	Key on service mode/F4 Boot from CD/Tape Select Maintenance Limited function Shell	ok boot -s	>boot Interact with IPL ? Y ISL>hpux -iS	{lilo} control-x linux S {grub} c kernel vmlinuz-2.4.9-13 single ro root=/dev/hda8 initrd	ok boot -s	> boot -fl s

				/initrd-2.4.9-13.img boot		
Maintenance mode		ok boot -as	>boot Interact with IPL ? Y ISL>hpux -lm		ok boot -as	
Interrupt Key			control-B		Stop-A	control-P
Return to console			co		ok go	
Timezone Management	/etc/environment /etc/profile	/etc/localtime	/etc/TIMEZONE	/etc/sysconfig/clock	/etc/TIMEZONE /etc/default/init	/etc/svid3_tz timezone
NTP Daemon	/etc/ntp.conf startsrc -s xntpd	/etc/rc.conf {xntpd_enable="YES"} /etc/rc.network	/etc/rc.config.d/netdaemons /sbin/init.d/xntpd	/etc/ntp.conf /etc/rc.d/init.d/xntpd	/etc/inet/ntp.conf /etc/init.d/xntpd	rcmgr set XNTPD_CONF YES /sbin/init.d/xntpd
Software	**AIX**	**FreeBSD**	**HP-UX**	**Linux RedHat**	**Solaris**	**Tru64**
Install Software	installp -a	pkg_add	swinstall	rpm -i package	pkgadd	setld -l
Uninstall software	installp -u	pkg_delete	swremove	rpm -e package	pkgrm	setld -d
List installed software	lslpp -L all	pkg_info -a	swlist	rpm -qa	pkginfo	setld -i
Verify	lppchk -v		swlist -l	rpm -V	pkginfo -i	setld -v

installed software			fileset -a state	package	pkginfo -p	
List all files	lslpp -f fileset	pkg_info -L package	swlist -l file fileset	rpm -ql package	pkgchk -l package	setld -i package
List installed patches	instfix -i		swlist -l patch what /stand/vmunix		patchadd -p	dupatch -track -type patch
Package owner	lslpp -w path		swlist -l file | grep path	rpm -qf file	pkgchk -l -p path	
SW Directory	/usr/lpp	/var/db/pkg	/var/adm/sw/	/var/lib/rpm	/var/sadm	/var/adm/smlogs
Devices	**AIX**	**FreeBSD**	**HP-UX**	**LINUX(RedHat)**	**SOLARIS**	**Tru64**
Devices	/dev	/dev	/dev	/dev	/devices	/dev
Install devices for attached peripherals	cfgmgr -v	/dev/MAKEDEV	insf -e	/dev/MAKEDEV	drvconfig devlinks disks tapes ports	scu scan edt scsimgr -scan_all
Remove device	rmdev -l		rmsf		rem_drv	
Device drivers	lscfg		lsdev		prtconf -D	
CPU	lsdev -Cc processor	sysctl hw.model	ioscan -fnC processor	cat /proc/cpuinfo	psrinfo -v	psrinfo -v
List Terminal	lsdev -Cc tty		ioscan -fnC tty		pmadm -l	
Diagnostics	diag	pciconf -l	stm	lspci pnpdump	/usr/platform/`uname	

					-m`/sbin/prtdiag ok test-all /opt/SUNWvts/bin/sunvts	
Whole Disk	/dev/hdisk#	/dev/ad0s1c	/dev/dsk/c#t#d0	/dev/sda	/dev/c#t#d0s2	/dev/rz0c
CDROM	/dev/cd0	/dev/acd0c	/dev/dsk/c#t2d0	/dev/cdrom	/dev/dsk/c#t6d0s2	/dev/rz3c
CDROM file type	cdrfs	cd9660	cdfs	iso9660	hsfs	cdfs
Rewinding tape drive	/dev/rmt0	/dev/rwt0d	/dev/rmt/0m	/dev/rst0 { c 9 0}	/dev/rmt/0	/dev/rmt0
Non-rewinding tape drive	/dev/rmt0.1	/dev/nrwt0d	/dev/rmt/0mn	/dev/nrst0 { c 9 128 }	/dev/rmt/0n	/dev/nrmt0
Floppy drive	/dev/rfd0	/dev/fd0	-	/dev/fd0	/dev/diskette	/dev/fd0c

Memory Usage

As indicated in earlier chapters, one of the main hardware elements for operation of a computer system is the RAM memory. This type of memory is characterized by its very fast access but the content of the data is temporary.

The operating system must handle physical memory to:
- Load more than one program in memory.
- Manage the execution of those programs that have not fit entirely in memory.
- Establish the relationship between logic and physical address of the programs loaded into memory.
- Share and manage the most efficient way possible the free and occupied space in memory.

When a program is executed, it is stored in memory. In the first UNIX systems there was a partition with a fixed size (2KB, 4KB, 8KB, etc.). In each of the partitions are stored a different program. However, this storage method limited the maximum number of programs that could run and did not use all available physical memory, which is known as fragmentation. Fortunately, technological change has meant that, at present, we can run more programs than can fit in physical memory. This is achieved through:
- The partition size is not fixed.
- It is not necessary that all partitions used by a program have to be arranged contiguously, since it is possible to locate all the necessary partitions using a complex addressing mechanism. To put it simply, we say that its function is to be inventoried PTBR address (or pointer to the page) or STBR (segment table) to find that piece of program you need at any given time.
- The programs that are resident in memory are able to share code, allowing to use less memory.
- Has appeared a secondary memory system, typically a hard disk, which is known as swap. This method allows to run programs larger than the physical memory, or which is available on it. The swap is part of what is known as

virtual memory. Into physical memory only stores a subset of all pages of a program. The rest is stored in the memory swap. This means that, at runtime, a program can get in and out of physical memory, which means that can be managed more effectively. In contrast, reading and writing data to disk is slower than when it is made directly in physical memory, which can represent a performance problem in our system. To write to disk operation is known as swap-out, while the read operation is called swap-in.

www.ingramcontent.com/pod-product-compliance
Lightning Source LLC
Chambersburg PA
CBHW080906170526
45158CB00008B/2016